Beh[ ] the Man!

A JOURNAL OF
SIMON OF CYRENE

By Father Martin De Porres

ISBN # 0-9648448-3-4
Library of Congress Catalog Card Number # 97-067802

© 1998 by CMJ Associates, Inc. Marian Publisher
P.O. Box 661 Oak Lawn, Illinois

Manufactured in the United States of America

CMJ ASSOCIATES, INC
Marian Publisher
P.O. Box 661
Oak Lawn, Illinois 60454

Introduction

The nail — Mother Mary's first gift to Simon of Cyrene, — had held the weight of her Son on the wooden cross. Simon had come to Jerusalem to visit friends, instead he began a life's journey to know and speak to all whoever had met this man, Jesus. Simon's repugnance for executions became a climb of compassion and deep reverence as he carried the prisoner's cross. He even seemed to be drawn to Jesus so much that heart spoke to heart.

Father Martin De Porres, captures the mysteries of the heart depicting Simon's journey of faith in the early Christian community. The apostle, John, presided over Simon's first Mass. Simon's First Communion was different than most Christians' for he saw not the hands of the priest, but the actual extended nail pierced hands of Jesus feeding him His very Body and His Blood.

Mysticism permeates this journal. The Upper Room, Pentecost, the baptisms of Simon's sons, Alexander and Rufus' families, his own ordination to the priesthood and his death reveal an intensity of the heart. Each of Simon's liturgical experience is set in mysticism and light, reflecting the author's tradition of the Orthodox Church. What refreshment for today's seeker!

Two themes intertwine in Simon's Cyrene's Journal: 1. The centrality of faith in the real Presence of Jesus in the Eucharist; and 2. Mother Mary's gentle, loving guidance and her simple, yet profound explanations of the mysteries of faith, especially of the priesthood which held Simon steadfast. Father Martin De Porres conveys his own great love of Mother Mary throughout the book. Mary is no staid person. She is alive, the kind of person you would want to meet and have as a friend.

Throughout the journal we observe Simon of Cyrene's transformation into the very heart of Jesus. Nowhere is this so evident than when Fabian, the jailer, beholds Simon of Cyrene, the martyr, illumined in a pillar of blazing light. BEHOLD THE MAN.

A Dear Friend

Dedication

Above all, this book is dedicated to

JESUS CHRIST,

for the guidance received from
His Eucharistic and Merciful Heart.

It is also dedicated to

my own mother, Theresa Yvonne Sherman.

From the beginning, He was and He knew me.
He gave me to you to nourish, so that I might
live and function as His and yours,
in order that I might give myself, on my own,
back to His arms that first cradled me before you.
Such a choice He made,
for no other mother could bring me back
to His arms as you.

Finally, it is dedicated to

Sister Charlotte Schaub, O.P.
Ed and Ginny Lopez
Palma Sumpman

and other very special people, who made this book possible
through their prayers and encouragement.

The Illustrator

The cover illustration was created by Joey Tolliver, an eighteen-year-old artist from Maryland, while visiting mutual friends of the author's in Twin Lake, Michigan. Father Martin De Porres met with his publisher, Jim Gilboy of CMJ Associates, Chicago, in November, 1995, at the Lopez family home. During their conversation they discussed cover design and their host suggested that Joey sketch a design. Father Martin described the story and within thirty minutes the cover was finished.

Father Martin states: *"Joey showed me several of his illustrations; primarily, comic book style. It was not the sort of thing I had in mind. For me, the cover had to be just right. It had to speak out and tell the magnitude of the event. Joey said that he had never tried that type of illustration and did not feel equal to it, but he would try. Within thirty minutes he returned from the other room with illustration in hand — a masterpiece. I have no doubt that his hand was guided from above. What we saw on the artist pad that day was a miracle, depicting the very essence of* **BEHOLD THE MAN.** *I believe Joey was sent to illustrate for us the strength, determination and compassion that we must **all** share in following Christ and upholding our brothers and sisters in Christ."*

Joey is from Bel Air, Maryland. He graduated from Harford Technical High School in 1995. Besides holding full time jobs in local restaurants to earn money for college, Joey acquired paramedic training and was an active member of the Abingdon Volunteer Fire Company and Rescue Squad since the age of 16. In August, 1996, he began his first formal art training at the AL COLLINS GRAPHIC DESIGN SCHOOL in Tempe, Arizona, where he is pursuing an associates degree in graphic communications.

The Author

Father Martin De Porres was born on May 7, 1950 in Detroit, Michigan. He attended Roman Catholic schools for the majority of his education, except eleventh grade when he attended public school.

In his early years Father developed a tremendous love for the Most Blessed Sacrament and the Blessed Mother, spending many hours in prayer before Our Lord in the tabernacle and attending Eucharistic Benediction as often as possible. This love has carried through to this day. Throughout the years he has organized Rosary groups among Roman Catholics, Eastern Orthodox and even Protestants.

Father Martin was ordained a priest on April 10, 1970, in a small Orthodox community in Texas. After the monastery closed, he traveled throughout the United States. In all his varied duties, he preached the Eucharist and the Rosary to anyone who would listen.

Father holds a doctorate in Divinity and is an associate of the Institute Of Religious Life. He also shares in the membership of the Marian Movement Of Priests. He conducts home liturgies and special services. Although he is semi-retired, Father Martin and his fellow religious, are endeavoring to obtain land and a building for a monastery that will be devoted to Perpetual Adoration of the Blessed Sacrament, under the care of the Little Brothers and Sisters of Jesus of the Most Blessed Sacrament. The proceeds from this and all future books will go to make their endeavor a reality by God's Holy Will.

TABLE OF CONTENTS

Foreword

Throughout the pages of the New Testament men and women are named their brief moment of fame in our salvations history. Simon of Cyrene is one of these:

And going out, they found a man of Cyrene, named Simon: him they forced to take up his cross. (Matthew 27: 32)

And they forced one Simon a Cyrenian, who passed by, coming out of the country, the father of Alexander and of Rufus, to take up his cross. (Mark 15: 21)

This is all we know of the man, Simon. Yet, in our meditative prayer we can ask ourselves: "What if?" and "How about?"

When we receive the Holy Eucharist, we receive the most precious, precious *Body* and *Blood* of our Jesus. The same Jesus whose cross Simon carried. This same precious *Blood* fell upon Simon, upon his hands, his clothing. This same precious *Body* leaned upon him for support. Surely, Simon was a changed man after his experience.

So begins a journey — a journey that explores Simon's faith, his feelings, his emotions — as he encounters those people who were a part of the life and ministry of Jesus. Through the Passion of Christ and his contact with the developing Christian community, Simon's love for his Lord deepens.

I invite you, my dear brothers and sisters, to ask yourselves, as Father Martin has done, "What if?" and "How about?"

Ginny Lopez
February 28, 1997

Prologue

I remember a bright and beautiful day when my cousin Simon came with the news. I was sitting under the large palm tree, keeping watch over my father's sheep. The sun was preparing its descent behind the sandy hills that lie beyond the river and green valley. There was such a calm in the air, like I have never felt before–so very much the opposite of Friday's terrible storm. The wind, gentle and cool after such a hot day, carried the last song of the birds, as evening began to cast its shadow. Such a peaceful time, that I wandered into deep soothing thought.

What had made this day so special, unlike other days? This first day of the week was so perfect. Suddenly, I heard a distant sound, stealing away my moments of solitude. Someone was calling my name. I turned and saw Simon running toward me. "Jacob! Jacob!" He hollered in great excitement. "Jacob! Did you hear what happened?" He was like a small child who needs to tell someone about something immediately or he will surely burst.

"Simon, calm yourself. What on earth is the matter? You look as if you're going to explode. Come. Sit with me and have some wine."

After a short time and almost a liter of sweet, mellow drink, Simon began his story.

CHAPTER 1

Behold The Man!

"Oh, Jacob! You should have been there! I never knew such a thing could happen. Certainly nothing that I could ever know. As usual, it was hot, and I decided to go to the city to visit friends. I never met with them because something tremendous was happening and the crowds were overbearing. The crowds were so thick, it was hard to get through to see what it was all about.

"It was more than just a crowd. It was an angry mob! *They were screaming murder!*

"They wanted the crucifixion of someone. Their eyes were wild with hate and their voices were vicious. Some were quiet. But then I saw the Temple guards put coins in their hands and they began to scream with a vengeance!

"Nearby was a small group of people. A few men and women who were sobbing. They were so immersed in their sorrow. They cried out in such shaky, pleading voices: 'He's innocent of any wrong! He is a man of peace, of love! Pardon him! Release him! *He's the Son of God!'*

"One of the women looked up at me. Our eyes met, causing a disturbance in my soul. Those eyes were penetrating. They caused my very soul to tremble. She was a woman of sorrow-but still, she radiated beauty, love. I was compelled to go to her and embrace her and hold her up under the weight of her pain. However, because of fear I hurried away. But in my mind's eye I could still see that beauty, so marred by sorrow. Why was she in such misery and what was her part in the ugliness going on in Jerusalem that day? It wasn't until later that I understood who she was.

"As I was listening to those who passed by me, I was able to piece together some of what was happening. It was the feast of

1

Passover, and according to Jewish custom, a prisoner would be released. There were two prisoners. One was a zealot, a man called Barabbas. He's a murderer and an enemy of the Roman authority. He was the one to be released. The other, a Nazorean named Jesus, was condemned in place of Barabbas.

"Jesus claimed to be the King of the Jews. They say He preached revolt. But yet He spoke only of love; even loving your enemy; even loving the Romans who have made us slaves in our own country.

"The man Barabbas preached revolt, also, but with weapons and death. I was so confused by how they could choose this zealot over a man of peace."

At this point, I commented, "I have heard of this Jesus. He was from Nazareth. I believe He's the Son of a carpenter. Well, anyway, continue your story."

"Jesus," Simon went on, "was made to carry a cross. I couldn't see because the crowd was so thick. At one point there was a little break in the crowd and I took my chance to move ahead some. I noticed that not all the people were part of that vengeful mob. I heard more and more good things about the Man. They said He could cure people *and make the dead rise!* There were reports of healing lepers, giving the blind their sight, curing a child from a distance. He supposedly even visited a friend who was dead *three days*, and brought him back to life. Many people saw this and can testify to it. The friend's name was Lazarus of Bethany. Jesus had caretakers roll back the stone to the grave. He entered the grave and bid Lazarus to come forward. *And he did!* Supposedly he's in better health now, than ever before. I just knew I had to see this Man, this Jesus.

"I continued to push through the crowd until I finally reached where He was. He had fallen under the weight of His cross. A woman took her veil and wiped the sweat and the blood from His face. I couldn't tell exactly what had happened, but the people near her kept pointing and looking to her veil. They were astonished.

"Oh, Jacob. The Roman soldiers kept pushing Him along and whipping Him with such brutality. It's their disgusting custom. Yet, with all the pain on His face, and the marks on His tortured, bloody body, His face showed so much love to all those He passed. The realization of how special this Man was, began to pierce my heart. A Man who suffered so much torture, and yet, had no hate or bitterness for anyone!

"As He staggered up the street, under the heavy weight of that cross, He passed a group of women who were weeping such bitter tears. There was so much noise, I couldn't hear all that was said except that they should weep for their children. Can you imagine? He was concerned about their children.

"Farther and farther He staggered. How was it possible for Him to keep going? What force of strength flowed through Him? Those who hated Him spit and threw stones at Him. Yet, He kept going. The woman I saw before, the one with the penetrating eyes, had caught up to Him. The soldiers tried to push her away at first, but then must have felt pity. They let her alone and briefly, she and Jesus looked in each others eyes with such love and compassion. Then I found out who she was. A woman exclaimed it was His *mother*!

"How sorrowful she was! How her heart must have been pierced with pain! To see her Son condemned and tortured so brutally. My own heart swelled with pain and compassion. No mother should be put through such anguish! No man should suffer like this! What crime should bear this cruelty? There certainly was something special about this woman. Her Son was a man beyond all men.

"At times I wanted to stop and go no further. How could I continue to witness this insanity? I pushed through the crowd as fast as I could, trying to get away from it all. My eyes were so full of tears, I could barely see. This Man was a *stranger* to me. Yet, I felt connected to Him. Why? How could that be possible?

"It was impossible to get through the crowd. I stopped for a moment and leaned against a wall. This was a street of sorrows. My heart wanted so much to reach out to Him. Oh, if I could have eased His pain just a little. My body became glued to the stone. If it had been possible to melt into the cracks of the wall, I would have.

"The procession came closer and closer. Not too far away, they stopped. Was His suffering over? Did He give up His spirit?

Was He dead? Perhaps peace had finally come to this remarkable Man. Maybe His mother was holding him in her arms. But then the procession started forward again. He must have fallen under the weight of the cross, as He had before.

"How was it possible that He could get up and continue? If only someone would help Him. If only *I* could help Him and relieve some of His torment.

"I saw Him plainly then. His eyes caught mine for just a moment. He started to fall once again, and the next thing I knew, a soldier had grabbed me away from my wall. He threw me with a tremendous force at Jesus, commanding *me* to carry the cross!

"Oh, I was frightened. But I chose not to resist. Did this Man somehow hear my thoughts. Could that be why I was chosen to carry His cross? "Once the cross was on my shoulder, He turned around, and I could see a faint smile through the blood from His brow, where the thorns, the *crown* He wore, had pierced Him. As we started to walk again, His mother was close. She nodded to me as if to say thank you. A soldier pushed her back, but her companions caught her so that she wouldn't fall. This mother had so much love for her Son. All mankind should have been blessed with such a mother!

"At times, Jesus walked next to me and though He said no words, I could feel Him speak to me, heart to heart. It was an inner understanding. One of my hands had blood on it. I noticed a lot of blood on that part of the cross. A *comfort* came over me that I am unable to describe. My body became warm and strong. The weight of the cross seemed less than before. All the pain I felt from its terrible weight was *gone*. I felt uplifted! Though it was heavy, it was not a burden. What magical power came over me? The closeness to Jesus was quickly becoming a kindred feeling. A mutual love was generating. This man was becoming like a brother. If He was my brother, then truly his mother was *my* mother. Later, I came to understand how this was to be.

"In the distance we could see the hill they call Golgotha, the Place of the Skull. Already there were two crosses with a space between. Perhaps that was to be for Jesus. Again the sorrow began to overwhelm me, for the stark reality could not be ignored. Truly,

I thought, my own heart would burst with the impending agony that awaited Jesus.

"I remember someone in the crowd called Him the Messiah. My heart said this was true and I believe the words of my heart. This Man was suffering for all of us. He was offering Himself up for all of us, in atonement for the sins we have committed against God and each other. He was giving us a chance to understand true brotherhood without reservation, a chance to live life to the fullest. Although I had never heard Jesus speak, my heart began to profess Him and to understand. He had been teaching me along the way while we walked. Though He did not speak for my ears to hear, He spoke to my heart.

"We finally arrived at the place of execution. I put the cross on the ground. I was free to walk away. But I couldn't. The soldiers pushed me away since I was no longer needed. I suppose I was in their way. If the opportunity had come, I think I would have volunteered to be crucified in His place. He looked at me and I moved slowly away. I realized that the love I had developed for Jesus would never leave, but would grow ever more intense. My heart and soul were captives of His love. I, Simon of Cyrene, a visitor to this city, came to visit some friends, and found the greatest Friend of all.

"How could I ever really know Him? Time was at an end. Looking over the crowd, I could see His mother. She could barely stand. A young man-maybe twenty five or so-was holding her up on one side, and a woman on the other side. I was captured by her face. Still so much sorrow, and yet, bearing some sort of knowledge kept in her heart. Without realizing my own movement, I was pressing through the crowd until I stood about ten feet from her. She was now half laying on the ground, cradled in the young man's arms. We were only about twenty feet from the cross.

"Meanwhile, the soldiers had stripped Jesus, laying Him on the cross. They tied Him to it so that His body would not fall when they raised it. I couldn't watch what came next. The scene would have been too hideous. I kept my eyes on His mother. But I knew each time she shuddered, that another nail was driven through those special hands that have healed so many. She never closed her eyes, but watched each miserable step as if a mystery was unfolding, that was hidden before. Then I slowly raised my eyes to Jesus as He was lifted upright, and with a bang, slid into place. There He was, in hideous pain with no way to relieve the tension of that pain. The soldier fastened a decree of condemnation to the top of the cross. What strange words-for they claimed Him to be *King Of The Jews*! "The sky had been cloudless all morning but now clouds slowly formed. I heard Him say something, but was too far away to understand His words. Some soldiers were off to the side and throwing dice for His garments. His mother and those with her began walking closer to the cross. One soldier-he who later pierced the side of Jesus-tried to stop them from coming closer. I ran to them and told the soldier that she was His mother. He allowed her to pass, and I took the opportunity to pass with them.

"We stood at the foot of the cross and saw so much blood running down His body, onto the cross and spattering on the ground. In His agony He spoke these words to His mother: *'Woman, behold thy son.'* (John 19:26) To the young man He said, *'Behold thy mother.'* (John 19:27)

"The young man was called John. They looked at each other briefly, as to say without words that they understood. In my heart I realized that she was now my mother also. That all of us would be her children. It was hard to understand, but easy to accept. His love for all people was so great that He wanted everyone to be a part of His family. Truly, I knew her now as my mother and Jesus, as my brother. Looking at her, I softly whispered the word *Mother*. The word sounded sweet to my ears and heart.

"I could not understand how He remained alive as long as He did. But even from the cross, He thought of others. He even forgave those who condemned Him. He asked His Father to forgive them because they did not understand what they were really doing. Even then, He *forgave* His *murderers*. One of the crucified criminals had taken pity on Jesus and asked Jesus to remember him. Jesus told him: *'Amen I say to thee, this day thou shalt be with me in paradise.'* (Luke 23:43)

"Finally, about the third hour, He raised His head and asked His Father to accept His spirit. At that moment, He bowed His head and died.

"Then a storm broke-thunder, lightening, torrents of rain. People were afraid and began to run away. The soldier took his spear and pierced the heart of Jesus. Blood and water burst forth, but Jesus was already dead. It was strange that they didn't break His legs, like the other two on either side of Him. Even the soldiers were afraid and the one who pierced Him said that this was the Son of God.

"I left and went to a quiet place to ponder all that I had seen. Finally, when the storm was over, I fell asleep."

"When I awoke, it was another day. I hurried to where Jesus was crucified. They had already taken Him down from the cross. My heart was sad, for I knew that I should never see Him again. Some people were still around, so I asked where He was taken. No one seemed to know. One lady said that He had been laid in His mother's arms. Then they carried Him away. She knew not where.

"I slowly walked back to the city and found that strange things had happened. A Levite told me that about the time of the storm's beginning, the curtain in the Temple had ripped in two somehow. Others said that even the dead rose and walked in the city. Some people were hiding behind their doors and the city was unusually quiet.

"I tried to find some of His Disciples. But no one knew where to look. Eventually, I walked out of the city and decided to come here to see you. Along the way, I grew weary and slept in a garden area.

"In the early morning hours, there was a powerful earth tremor that woke me with a fright. A soldier ran past me with a look of terror. He yelled out something hysterically. It sounded like he said, *'He is risen from the dead! HE'S ALIVE!'*

"I searched for the tomb all over, and then, suddenly, I saw it! The stone was rolled away. No guards were to be seen. Although I did not understand what happened, I felt like rejoicing. The hysterical soldier said that *He* was alive! I remember that some people, before the crucifixion, said that in three days He would rise. And then they laughed. I paid no more attention to it. Now I understand."

"For those who believe, no explanation is necessary. For those who do not believe, no explanation is possible. All I know is that I went to the city to visit friends. Instead, I found Jesus, my Friend and my God. Though I never really got to know Him or to spend time with Him, He will always be with me. Someday we will walk along side each other again. Not on a road of misery, but along a rambling brook that runs through the garden of life. To think that I, Simon of Cyrene, was blessed to carry His cross. Now I can spend the rest of my days in joy. No matter what may be strewn in my path, I will always know His comfort. From now until the end of my life, I shall seek out and learn from those who knew Him. Praised be Jesus, true God and true man. So be it!"

CHAPTER 2

They Shared His Meal

Some time has passed since the evening I visited cousin Jacob while he tended his sheep in the valley. I've heard that Jesus was seen in Jerusalem by many people, that He has walked and talked with several of them. Are these reports given by the weak minded who are subject to hallucinations? Or is it true? Is He still very much alive? My heart, my very soul, believes that He is risen from the dead. Perhaps if I had not had the privilege of sharing His cross, I would not believe. Even amid the horrors of our day, brought upon us by our Roman persecutors, my heart knows a blessed joy that surpasses these evils.

I spent several days with Jacob before returning to Jerusalem. On the way I came upon a woman, Joanna, who gave me an account of meeting the Lord. She was one of several women who had gone to the tomb and found it empty. She was most willing to tell me of her experience. Of course, I was most anxious to hear of it. Every word that could be spoken about Jesus would be like finding an oasis with cool water, after traveling through a parched, lifeless desert. Since the day was very hot and her account was long, she led me over to a large tree, where we sat in the coolness of its shade.

Joanna took out a loaf of bread and a decanter of wine from the bundle she carried. We shared the bread after the blessing, and she remarked, "Whenever I share bread with friend or stranger, I remember that last meal we ate with the Lord. If you like, I'll tell you of that night, but first I want to tell you about His recent appearances." She spoke with sincerity and devotion, as if in prayer, while recounting her remarkable tale.

"Jesus was laid in the tomb late in the day as the Sabbath fast approached. So as to follow the Law of Moses, we decided to come back afterward to anoint His body. The tomb was sealed but we hoped someone would roll back the stone for us.

"It was the first day of the week and nearly dawn, when we arrived at the tomb. The stone was *already* rolled back. Upon entering the tomb, we found it empty! Mary of Magdala burst into tears: 'Who has stolen the body of my Lord?'

"I fell to the ground, for there was no strength left in my legs to hold me up. How could they take His body from us? Haven't they caused Him and us enough degradation and pain? Must they take his precious body away, too?

"Mary, the mother of James, told us to keep still and to look through our tears at the angelic figures before us! Magdala and I were so upset at what happened that we were blinded from all else. Mary always had better control over her emotions. When we realized what she was saying, we, too, saw these Angels, all aglow. Terrified, we bowed to the ground.

"The Angels spoke, *'Why do you seek the living with the dead. He is not here, but is risen. Remember how He spoke unto you, when He was yet in Galilee, saying: the Son of Man must be delivered into the hands of sinful men, and be crucified, and the third day rise again.'* (Luke 24:5-7)

"Shamefully, we remembered these prophetic words of our Lord. How could we not remember His statement?" Joanna, with tears in her eyes, related how the others did not believe their story. Her sadness was due to her own failure to recognize what had taken place. I tried to console her and a hint of a smile appeared on her face.

We sat in the shade of the tree, eating bread and drinking wine, when a man came walking toward us. He was a small man, thinly built. Joanna leaned toward me, saying, "This is Simeon. It was in his house that we had that last meal with our beloved Master. He, too, is a follower of Jesus since that night."

We invited Simeon to sit and break bread with us. He accepted, cheerfully exclaiming, "Oh, but the day is hot and the air is dry. This shade is refreshing. The breeze lessens the sting of the heat."

Joanna offered him wine, which he savored gratefully, holding it in his mouth to soak up the dryness. She introduced us and a new friendship began. I told Simeon what Joanna had said about the Lord choosing his house for the Passover Meal. I said I would love to know more about that night. Simeon was more than willing to share his memory, and he began his account, excitement in his voice.

"Oh that the Lord should have chosen me and my house to be so blessed! That day was much like this one and the streets were crowded because of the Passover preparations. I had gone to the well near the gate of the city to fill my water jar. I was pouring the water into my jar when two strangers came to drink. There was a strange feeling in my stomach, as if I knew them. It was just past noon.

"As I walked back to my house, a sense of being followed overwhelmed me, although I felt no fear. I entered my dwelling, leaving the door open. "In a few moments, the two men came inside. They introduced themselves as Peter and John, Disciples of Jesus. Peter was tall, a burly man with a full, curly beard-perhaps in his forty-second year. John was younger, maybe twenty three, smooth faced with a slender build and average height. Peter spoke, 'The Teacher asks you: ""Do you have a guest room where I may eat the Passover with My Disciples?""'

"I told him that I had an upstairs room that would be ideal. Little did I know at that time, the full impact of what would happen that night. We embraced as brothers and they left. A few hours later they returned with everything needed for the celebration of the Passover, the day of Unleavened Bread and the sacrifice of the paschal lamb. Once they had everything set, they invited me to share their meal — that the Master would wish it. My heart filled with joy."

Joanna spoke up: "Many of us women were also invited to the meal by Mary, the Lord's mother. We went to be of service and to share the meal. We were there early and Mary instructed us. Peter was very demanding and authoritative but then that is his way. When he was too overbearing, Mary would look at him, and he seemed to melt, smiling with the gentleness of a kitten. Mary has a gentleness about her that could tame a savage beast. She hummed a little tune while working and her smile never seemed to fail. I dropped a special bowl, already purified but now conta-minated. Mary picked it up and told me not to worry, that she would prepare another. She placed her arm around me like a lov-ing mother. Her eyes were so full of love. She treated us all as if we were her very own children. She emulated the Master in so many ways.

"As we set the table and Mary placed the bread and wine in their proper place, something came over her. It was a look I've never seen on her before. Her light-hearted smile turned to a sad, far-off look. Her beautiful blue eyes swelled with tears. She just stood there looking at the bread and wine. How I wished I knew what troubled her and how to console her. She's always there for us; yet, we were too blind to realize what she already knew.

"The Lord usually spoke in parables and many of us found it difficult to understand their full meanings. John, on the other hand, always so full of compassion and love, saw through every-one and knew when consolation was needed. Like Mary, he gave unceasingly of himself for the others. John fit right in with Jesus and Mary. He could have been Mary's own son and brother of the Lord. At the cross it was no wonder that Jesus entrusted His moth-er to John."

Simeon added: "Mary must have known the *new* meaning of the bread and wine; she must have suspected what would happen that night. We sat at table with the Twelve closest to Jesus and the women served, as that is our custom. Jesus was His usual self; there was no hint of the events yet to come. Although I remember that His mother came and poured some water for us. When she came to Jesus, they looked into each other's eyes. Mary placed her free hand over her heart, and Jesus said softly, 'I love you very much, Mother; yet, another sword must pierce your heart.'"

Joanna, remembering that moment, said, "The looks on their faces were so very tender. It was then that Judas, that betrayer, entered the room. Jesus' eyes left His mother's face and followed him until Judas took his place nearby. Judas was extremely uncomfortable, as if he had much on his mind."

Simeon interrupted, shouting, "And why shouldn't he feel uncomfortable? He was about to betray our Master! He must already have been plotting to find a way to hand him over."

I could tell Simeon was very upset at this memory of the man Judas Iscariot, and rightly so. Offering him more wine, I asked Joanna to continue her account. Simeon calmed down and bowed his head, as if silently to ask forgiveness for his outburst.

"Judas Iscariot did not stay long," Joanna continued, "for the Lord spoke to him quietly and he left with bewilderment on his face. Opening the door, he looked back as if he wanted to say something. Instead, he bowed his head and left. Only Jesus knew why he left so early. We thought the Master had sent him on an errand. If we had known, we could have stopped him. But destiny was not ours to control. The supreme act of love that Jesus would fulfill was unchangeable. It was the most heroic gift that the Father could bestow on His children.

"We were like one huge family that night, sharing ideas, hopes and dreams, and the joy of the Passover. How God loves His people, unworthy as we are. John, the youngest, whom Jesus loved most, became tired and rested his head on Jesus' shoulder. I think he could easily have fallen asleep but at this point Jesus became very somber. His face grew sad and a tear slipped down his cheek. Those who noticed the change began to nudge the others. John sat up. Mary, the mother of Jesus, sat down, holding a wine jug from which she was filling goblets. She simply stared at her son, a tear running down her own cheek. Did she know what was about to happen?"

Calm now, Simeon took up the account, describing what the Master said and did with the bread and wine. "While we were yet eating, Jesus became quiet, sad. I remember He gazed about the room, His eyes falling on each of us. On His left cheek, a tear disappeared into the thick hair of His beard. As the others noticed this change, they grew quiet. It was then that He stood up and raised His eyes toward Heaven, remaining motionless for several minutes. Then, lowering His eyes, He bent down and picked up the loaf of bread. After offering it to the Father and blessing it, He broke it, gave it to the disciples on either side of Him and said, *'Take ye and eat. This is my body.'* (Matt. 26:26) Slowly the bread was passed from one to another until all partook. Although we really did not understand the meaning of His words, we were filled with a stirring in our souls.

"The Master then picked up the goblet of wine, the one kept as the Elijah Cup, and again looking up to Heaven, He spoke to the Father. He trembled slightly. Although He held the goblet securely, it appeared weighty. Another tear fell, this time into the wine. Raising His eyes and scanning the entire room, He held the goblet out to us and said, *'Drink ye all of this. For this is my blood of the new testament, which shall be shed for many unto remission of sins.'* (Matt. 26:27-28) He paused, swallowing hard, and continued, *'And I say to you, I will not drink from henceforth of this fruit of the vine, until that day when I shall drink it with you new in the kingdom of my Father.'* (Matt. 26:29)

Joanna offered us more cool wine. The sun had shifted from its original position. Simeon suggested that we come to his house before the sun made its descent into night. Joanna explained that she needed to go on to her own house, for she had much to do before sunset, and begged us to excuse her.

After we bid Joanna a blessed evening, Simeon and I walked to his house. The closer we came, the more my own heart swelled with emotion. Soon I would be in the very room where Jesus and His Mother and the Disciples were gathered together for the last time. This is where He ate His last meal with them.

As we walked, we both pondered within ourselves all that had been discussed with Joanna over the past several hours. It was strange, for I felt like I had just parted with my sister and was walking with my brother. We were bonded to each other like blood relatives. Perhaps the new Blood we share in Jesus unites us as a new family, a family that surpasses our birth family, for now we are reborn into the family of Jesus.

"Here we are," exclaimed Simeon as we approached the doorway to a plain structure. When we entered, Simeon sent his servant for fresh water, bread and a flask of wine.

When we had refreshed ourselves, Simeon offered to show me the upper room. My heart was pounding as I followed him, knowing that I would be blessed to be in the very room in which Jesus shared His final meal with those He loved. I would have given my very life to be present on that night. Had I the pleasure of knowing Him these past years, my joy would have been complete. For now I must be content to learn of Him from those who knew and served Him. This is my quest.

As we came to the top of the stairs, Simeon opened the door to a large room with a long, low table. On the table was placed a long covering, folded several times. There appeared to be something wrapped within. The room was very clean, simply furnished and properly arranged. Compared to the rest of the house, this room was kept very special. Simeon could see the wonder on my face, so he volunteered the answer before I had a chance to ask.

"This, my friend, is the way the women left the room after the Lord and the Disciples went to the Mount of Olives. His mother placed the goblet, plate, napkin and other items He used within the table covering, keeping them as a remembrance of that special night. Here is the towel He used to dry the feet of His friends and the scroll of the Passover readings. I have not had the heart to move them from here. Someone will come for them and take them to His mother."

I wanted to see these treasures but didn't dare to ask. Simeon continued to describe the entire scene from that night. He showed me where Jesus sat, and as best he could recall, everyone else. His description was so detailed and powerful, I felt like I was transported back in time to that night. It was so real that my eyes seemed to behold all that transpired, like a vision. I could no longer distinguish between Simeon's description and what I was seeing and hearing.

I believe that the Master, the Lord Himself, favored me with more than a glimpse of that night, actually taking me there. I could see and hear Him. Our eyes met. My heart beat faster and harder than before. My whole body tingled. The words He spoke are written on my heart for all times. All that He said was important and overwhelming, but *these* words meant so much to me: *"Let not your heart be troubled. You believe in God: believe also in me. In my Father's house there are many mansions. If not, I would have told you: because I go to prepare a place for you. And if I shall go, and prepare a place for you, I will come again, and will take you to myself; that where I am, you also may be.* (John 14:1-3) *If you love me, keep my commandments. And I will ask the Father, and he shall give you another Paraclete, that he may abide with you for ever.* (John 14:15-17) *The spirit of*

truth . . . I will not leave you orphans; I will come to you.
(John14:18) *. . . Peace I leave with you, my peace I give unto
you.* (John 14:27) *. . . If you abide in me and my words abide in
you, you shall ask whatever you will, and it shall be done unto
you. In this is my Father glorified; that you bring forth very
much fruit, and become my disciples. As the Father hath loved
me, I also have loved you. Abide in my love. If you keep my commandments, you shall abide in my love; as I also have kept my
Father's commandments and do abide in his love.* (John 15:7-
10)

*"These things I have spoken to you, that my joy may be in
you, and your joy may be filled. This is my commandment, that
you love one another, as I have loved you. Greater love than this
no man hath, that a man lay down his life for his friends. You are
my friends, if you do the things that I command you.* (John 15:11-
14) *. . . You have not chosen me: but I have chosen you; and have
appointed you, that you should go, and should bring forth fruit;
and your fruit should remain: that whatsoever you shall ask of
the Father in my name, he may give it you. These things I command you, that you love one another.* (John 15:16-17)

*"These things I have spoken to you, that in me you may
have peace. In the world you shall have distress: but have confidence, I have overcome the world."* (John 16:33)

His words are truly burnt deep in my heart. He spoke directly to me and to all who would listen to them. I have been includ-
ed among His Disciples, to go and bear fruit, bringing all into this
wonderful family. I knew when I carried His cross for Him that I
was to be a part of His family. What joy, what everlasting joy!

When I realized that I was still in the room with Simeon, it
was due only to the fact that he was shaking my shoulder and calling my name. "What happened? I thought you had died; yet, you
were standing," Simeon exclaimed. "You were hardly breathing
but your face was aglow."

I told him what happened and he said, "Many have been
touched by the Master in very special ways. Once we allow Him
into our lives and open our hearts to Him, He joins Himself to us
and lives in us. There is a very special time when He comes in a
most intimate way.

"Remember earlier when we broke bread with Joanna and we spoke of how it reminded us of this place and that last meal? Well, it is that time when we come together to commemorate the actual meal of the Lord that the intimacy of Christ fills us and draws us closer together. Jesus told us to do this often in remembrance of Him. Therefore, small groups of us gather together with one of the Apostles to commemorate the meal. We must do it in hiding for fear of the authorities. When we come together, we praise the Father and sing psalms. We listen to the Word of God from the Torah and are taught the teachings of the Master, Our Lord, Jesus the Christ. Then we break the bread and drink of the cup. It is our belief, our *conviction*, that we must do as He commanded us. When we eat of the bread, it is His very Body that we eat. When we drink of the cup, it is His very Blood that we drink. It is when we do this that we receive the fullness of Him. We are joined with Him in a oneness, a completeness. It is a force that unites us all to Him and to each other. When we receive Him in the bread and the wine, His Body and Blood, we are convicted and renewed, willing to do all and risk all for His sake. Our hearts fill with a burning love for Him and each other. Forgiveness is an act of love. While on the cross He said, *'Father, forgive them, for they know not what they do.'* (Luke 23:34) He forgave even the cruel tormentors who crucified Him. He laid down His life for you and for me. The world shall never have such a friend as the Lord again. Yet He is still with us. He is with us in this Remembrance, and He will always be with us as we continue to do His command." Simeon was so right.

I had an opportunity to be present at one of the gatherings with an Apostle. When it came time to partake of the bread and wine, I, too, believed all that Simeon had said.

On that particular morning I went out to a nearby stream, where several people had gathered, enjoying the water. Once we were in the coolness of the water, I could hear and see what was being done. Though similar to what John the Baptizer did before his untimely murder, there was a difference. These people were being baptized in the Name of Jesus, the Son of God. I wanted this baptism and so I approached the Disciple Jacob to ask if I might have it.

Jacob said, "Jesus the Christ has brought you to this. He has called you unto Himself. Kneel, Simon of Cyrene, and pray that God, through His Son, will renew you. *By this pouring on of water, I baptize you in the Name of the Father, and of the Son, and of the Holy Spirit.* Rise! On this day you are reborn. Go and remain sinless."

At that moment my soul was flooded with an overwhelming joy and sense of belonging.

Later in the evening, being invited to a special gathering, I was to partake of the Sacred Meal, the Breaking of the bread, the sharing of the very Body and Blood of Jesus Christ. The Apostle John, he who was so loved by the Lord, would be leading the gathering of believers. John was the one who stood faithfully with Mary, the mother of Jesus, at the foot of her Son's cross. It was to John, his faithful Disciple, that Jesus entrusted the care of His mother. The other Apostles were afraid and stayed far from the site of execution. I can still see that awesome event as though it had just happened.

The gathering was to take place in the home of the widow Claudia. She lived on the outskirts of Jerusalem and was well liked by the authorities, who had no idea that she was a follower of Jesus. Her home would be safe. As I walked through the streets of Jerusalem, I was aware of anyone who might follow me. After all, the authorities were trying to find us and stamp us out of existence. The closer I came to Claudia's house, the more intense was my awareness.

I knocked lightly on the door. A man answered and asked, "Whom do you wish to see?"

My response was coded: "The fish in the sea are plentiful."

With that he let me enter and guided me through the large and exquisite villa. We passed through several rooms, arriving at a garden filled with colorful and exotic flowers. A very high wall surrounded the garden and connected to the villa, offering safe surroundings. In the center of the courtyard, sixty or more people were gathered. The scene was humbling. Men, women and children intermingled, standing or sitting on the ground or on benches. Mothers and fathers held their children in tender embrace. Husbands and wives stood close to one another, a bond of unity between them. They were all in prayer, old and young, rich and poor, all together as a family, the family in Jesus. I was introduced to Claudia and a few others who made me feel at home. I knelt to offer my thanks for my new family.

Moments later Claudia addressed the crowd: "My brothers and sisters in Jesus the Christ, we have with us today, two very special people. The Apostle John, upon whom the Lord showed His favor, will speak to us and offer up the Body and Blood of our Risen Lord. The mother of Jesus is also with us tonight. How very blessed we are!"

The Apostle John and Mary greeted us. Once again I saw the scene at Calvary. The faces on John and Mary were not the same as I remembered. Instead of sad and despairing, they were joyful, radiant. There seemed to be a glow coming forth from them. Seeing me, Mary came to my side, turned to all and said, "This is Simon, who helped Jesus carry the heavy cross. He is a follower, too. He is our brother. As we have opened our hearts to each other, through Jesus, let us now receive him as one of us."

She then turned back to me, calling me her adopted son. I remember how she stood in such agony beneath the cross, witnessing the degradation, desolation and death of the One she brought into the world and intensely loved. She heard the blasphemies and reviling of the priests and the people, but her faith did not die. If Calvary was our Lord's crown of sorrow, it was also Mary's; yet, how courageous she was. Others sat and watched the suffering Christ, or beat their breasts and cried; but Mary stood by the cross. Should she not have been spared the agony of seeing the Son of her womb die such a despicable death? No! It was in the divine order of things that she should be found beneath that cross to receive the parting blessing of her Son and Savior, and His committal of her to the affectionate care of John, the Apostle whom He loved.

"Blessings and greetings be upon this house," John began, "and on all who gather here to remember the Sacred Meal of Christ's Body and Blood as He commanded us; and especially to Claudia, who offers all for the sake of Christ and this gathering. In truth, I love each of you and all who have come to know the truth. This love is based on the truth that abides in us and will be with us forever. In truth and love, then, we shall have grace, mercy and peace from God the Father and from Jesus Christ, the Father's Son."

John spoke for some time and then led us in prayer and in psalms of praise. One of the men brought forth a scroll and read from it. The reading was from Isaiah the prophet:

> *I the Lord have called thee in justice,*
> *and taken thee by the hand,*
> *and preserved thee.*
> *And I have given thee for a covenant of the people,*
> *for a light of the Gentiles:*
> *That thou mightest open the eyes of the blind,*
> *and bring forth the prisoner out of prison,*
> *and them that sit in darkness*
> *out of the prison house.*
> *I the Lord, this is my name:*
> *I will not give my glory to another,*
> *nor my praise to graven things.*
> *The things that were first,*
> *behold they are come:*
> *and new things do I declare:*
> *before they spring forth,*
> *I will make you hear them.* (Isaiah 42:6-9)

John spoke again and gave us an account from the Savior's life, of which he was witness: "On our second tour of Galilee, the Lord prepared us for the work that lay ahead of us. When He finished instructing us, our Lord sent us forth to gather the harvest by preaching and teaching, while He returned to Capernaum. On His journey He received the sad news that John the Baptizer had been beheaded by Herod. What sorrow must have flooded His heart when He heard of John's death!

"Soon we returned, bubbling with enthusiasm in our accounts of our mission. We looked forward to the Master's commendation and to His further advice. The crowds, however, were as demanding as ever, and Jesus suggested that we take a ship to a desert place to rest. But there was no escape. The crowds followed and met us on the shore where we landed. The Lord's heart was touched by the devotion of the people and so He went ashore and preached to them. Here He worked the miracle of the loaves and fishes. So great was their enthusiasm that the crowds wanted to make Him their king. He bade us sail for Bethsaida. Then He dismissed the admiring throng. That night He walked over the water to join us as we sailed.

"We landed on the coast, south of Magdala, and the word of His coming spread through all the surrounding villages. Many sick and lame came to us and many remained waiting in the villages for the Lord to heal them. As He went His way from village to village, He let loose the whole force of His healing power, lavishing His goodness on all, that they might see Him as the Messiah, God's own Son.

"From there Christ went back to Capernaum, and the throng that He miraculously fed with a few loaves and fishes the day before, crowded into the synagogue to hear Him preach. He fed them miraculously on the previous day to prepare *them* for a much greater miracle, and *us* for this night and other nights to come. *'. . . I am the living bread which came down from heaven.'* (John 6:51) He said, but many could not accept this and found it overwhelming and heartbreaking. Protesting that this was too much to accept, the crowd melted away, refusing to give Him their faith. He had told them, *'He that eateth my flesh, and drinketh my blood, hath everlasting life: and I will raise him up in the last day.'* (John 6:55) He meant this quite literally, but they resented His words and left. They understood like you, but unlike you, they did not believe. Christ, therefore, let them go. All of you He holds close to His heart."

After his sermon, John went to the table prepared with a white cloth, goblet and a plate with a loaf of bread. The goblet was the one in Simeon's home, the very one that Jesus had used. Of course! Mary had brought it.

The Apostle began to pray intensely to the Father. Then he picked up the bread and prayed, "Blessed are You, Lord, God of all creation. Through Your goodness we have this bread to offer, which earth has given and human hands have made. It will become for us the bread of life."

He picked up the Goblet and prayed, "Blessed are You, Lord, God of all creation. Through Your goodness we have this wine to offer, fruit of the vine and work of human hands. It will become our spiritual drink."

We praised God in song and we prayed and John spoke once more: "On the first day of the feast of Unleavened Bread, Peter, Andrew and I went up to Jesus and asked Him where we were to prepare for the Passover supper. The Lord told us to go to a man in the city, one Simeon whom you all know and love, and tell him: *'The master saith to thee; Where is the guest chamber, where I may eat the pasch with my disciples?'* (Luke 22:11)

"We did as Jesus requested and prepared the Passover supper. Many gathered for this meal. Our venerable mother Mary took charge to see that everything was in order. This goblet that we use tonight is the same goblet that the Lord Himself used on that Holy Thursday that we are commemorating."

Every word that John spoke burned into my heart, and with every beat of it, there was a new surging of love. He led us in the prayer Jesus taught us when the people asked Him to teach us how to pray:

> *Our Father who art in heaven,*
> *hallowed be thy name.*
> *Thy kingdom come.*
> *Thy will be done*
> *on earth as it is in heaven.* (Matt. 6:9-10)

Your will be done! Yes, Father, in my life let me be submissive to Your Holy and Divine Will. Let my whole life be an extension of Your work in this world, so plagued with evil. I want so to receive every day, the Holy Bread, given to us by Your Son. I am nothing, Lord, except what You would wish me to be. Help me to forgive all who have ever trespassed against me, for how dare I ask Your forgiveness when I am not willing to do the same. Deliver me, O Lord, and keep me in Your loving hands, free from all evil.

I felt as if this prayer was becoming alive in me. Only this morning I found a new freedom in baptism, and yet my entire life seemed to be maturing in one day.

"My friends," John addressed us, "we are now going to offer up the bread and wine as Jesus did just weeks ago."

This was to be the moment for which I longed. Now I would be at the precious Sacred Meal. I knew that the bread of which I would partake, would be His very Body, and the wine, His very

Blood. This was the very proclamation of Jesus Himself. This truth would be handed down through the ages yet to come. For truth is truth and cannot change-Divine truth that will feed us with all we shall ever need. Soon I would glimpse the very Christ I've come to love more than my own life. I would share with all the believers that most precious and awesome gift given to us by the Father.

John continued, "When the hour arrived, He took His place at table, and all of us with Him. During the meal, Jesus took the bread, blessed it, broke it and gave it to those assembled, saying, *'Take ye and eat. This is my body.'* (Matt. 26:26)

I fell to my knees and then prostrated myself on the ground *for Jesus appeared before us.* The bread was no longer present, but *Jesus Himself stood before us.* Even John went to his knees.

In His hands were the marks of the nails and on His head, the traces of the crown of thorns. He was radiant, brighter than the sun. Yet, we could see Him plainly. *He* then took the goblet, gave thanks and raised it up, saying, *"Drink ye all of this. For this is my blood of the new testament, which shall be shed for many unto remission of sins. And I say to you, I will not drink from henceforth of this fruit of the vine until that day when I shall drink it with you new in the kingdom of my Father."* (Matt. 26:27-29)

Our eyes remained on the bread and wine; no, rather the very Body and Blood of our Risen Savior. Our hearts were lifted up and our eyes filled with tears of supreme joy. Mary, His mother, took me by the hand and led me like a small child to the holy Table of the Lord. My whole body felt as though it was as light as a feather. Was I floating or were my feet actually touching the ground. My heart beat faster and faster, but without any sense of discomfort, only profound love.

Mary received the Body and Blood from the hands of John, after she knelt and bowed in humble respect and devotion. She was radiant and the Sacred Bread seemed to glow as she received It. I was next, and as I saw this most awesome gift come toward me, *the hands of Christ Himself* gave it to me, for the hands bore the marks of the nails. My very soul cried out in ecstasy and praise. I heard the sweet sound of the angelic chorus all around me. I have seen my precious, Risen Lord. I have partaken and shared in His most precious Body and Blood. I have been higher than the tallest mountain. I have walked in Heaven itself. Praised be the Lord. . . .

CHAPTER 3

His Mother Remembers

Several weeks passed since the time the Apostles moved into Simeon's house. The upper room was a safe haven and Simeon offered his home for as long as they should have need of it. Peter, James and Andrew often went together to the Temple to praise God.

The other Apostles joined them on various occasions but it was decided that they would not go as a group. It was far too dangerous since the authorities still searched for them. It was much safer and wiser to stay and meet in the upper room.

Only the chosen ones knew where the Apostles stayed. Many of Jesus' friends gathered there to praise the Lord. The mother of Jesus, who was living in the home of the Apostle John, came nearly every day with him to be with the chosen ones. Everyone awaited their arrival with great anticipation.

The mother of Jesus had adopted all of us as her very own. In word and love, she calls us the brothers and sister of Jesus. We feel very free to call her our mother.

I remember when Mary and John came to the home of the widow Claudia, where I first joined in the *Breaking of the Bread,* our Holy Mother said of me, "This is Simon, who helped Jesus carry the heavy cross. He is a follower, too. He is our brother. As we have opened our hearts to each other, through Jesus, let us now receive him as one of us."

I, Simon of Cyrene, was counted as one of her adopted sons. She became the mother of us all. Many times we would sit at her feet and listen to the memories only she could tell as His mother. With such tenderness she recounted the childhood of Jesus.

Around dusk the other day, I went to visit the Apostles and other brethren to bring them needed supplies. Thomas, the one who, after the Resurrection, placed his finger into the wounds of Jesus in order to believe, greeted my knock at the door. After taking the supplies and placing them on a nearby chair, we greeted one another with a holy kiss as the Lord had taught us.

Thomas exclaimed, "His mother is here with John and has asked about you. Andrew told her that you would arrive soon. She knows how much you want to hear about the Master so she chose to wait until you arrived.

"Mary, Joanna and the other women are preparing a meal for everyone so we have plenty of time. Lazarus, the friend whom Jesus raised from the dead, and his two sisters, are with us as well. Martha told me that she wants to sit at Mother Mary's feet and listen concerning Jesus. She wants to share in the good part. Come, let's go up and join them."

Once in the upper room, John and Joseph of Arimathea, in whose tomb Jesus had been laid, came over and greeted me. "Mother Mary wanted to know when you arrived," John said. "She has something for you. She's in the kitchen with the other women."

There was a new face among the brethren. Joseph caught the direction of my look and said, "That is Mirianna, the mother of Judas of Iscariot. She arrived early this morning with Joanna. It's the first time she has approached any of us since that day. Her heart has been so heavy with sorrow for what her only son did. We tried to console her but nothing could stop her flood of tears. Her whole body shakes with remorse."

John spoke up: "It reminds me of the painful sorrow Mother Mary suffered as she stood beneath Jesus' cross. As I held her in my arms, every part of her body trembled. Her tears flowed from her swollen eyes, covering her face as she pressed her hand against her pain-pierced heart. She became so weak that she could not stand. I guided her to the ground, bracing her against my body, and held her just as she later held Jesus when He was taken down from the cross."

"Mirianna shares this tremendous pain, but in a different way," Joseph began. "Some time after she arrived, Mother Mary and John spotted Mirianna. Mother Mary started toward her, but when Mirianna saw her coming, she fell to her knees and screamed out, 'Have mercy, have mercy!' Mary was filled with such compassion for her. She fell to her own knees, embracing the poor mother of him who betrayed her own Son. She held her ever so tenderly for quite a while, and then spoke to Mirianna: 'My dear, dear sister, Mirianna, do not weep so. My Son has heard your tears of sorrow and embraces you with the same tenderness that holds you now. You have not sinned, nor should you share, in any way, the responsibility of Judas' actions. I feel sadness for the loss of your only son. I know the pain and sorrow that holds on to you. We share this in our losses. You have asked for mercy and forgiveness. Know that you have merited this through your tears.'

"Mary then took Mirianna's face in her hands and raised it so that they could look into each other's eyes and said, 'As the mother of Jesus, Who was crucified for you and for me, I forgive your son for the part he played in my Son's Passion and Death. "'But that is not the end. Jesus is alive! He has resurrected as He promised, and someday we, too, will be resurrected and live with Him in the promise of the glory of His Father. I love you-just as my Son loves you. Come. Be a part of our family. Let a new you, prepared for us by the Father, fill the emptiness you now feel and give you new life. . . .'

"How beautiful was the mother of our Master. There was no bitterness in her-only love and compassion for the mother of the son who betrayed her Son, even unto the kiss of death. Of all humans, she is the truest example of all that her Son taught."

The women, who had prepared a simple meal of vegetables and lamb, called us all to sit at table and to share the meal. They never knew exactly how many would be at the meal, but there was always enough. This day about eighty friends were present.

Peter remarked to John, "It is like the multiplication of the loaves and fishes all over again. Those who are in need, are always free to take the leftovers home." How very true this was for we always ended up with more than we started.

After the meal Mother Mary walked across the room and sat, relaxing in a chair. She appeared to be so tired, and yet, ready to serve in any way that might be asked of her. It wasn't long before

Lazarus, Mary and Martha were sitting on the floor near her, chatting. Others joined them and soon all of us were gathered like children, waiting to hear a story from our mother.

Although Mary was fatigued, she became alert and rested as she began to tell her memories of the early days. There was a real gleam in her eyes when she began speaking about the birth of her Son and the events leading up to it. As she spoke, our attention grew more and more intense, and we held on to every word.

Mother Mary recalled, "One morning, while Mother and Father were at market, I remained to tidy up the house. It was such a beautiful day with a gentle breeze blowing through the window openings. The children could be heard playing in the street and little Sarah, from down the street, was sitting outside, under the window, singing a child's song to the Father. She loved to sit there with her doll because she enjoyed listening to the Psalms of King David that I sang to praise the Lord. She would learn some of the phrases of the Psalms in this way and sing them throughout the day. She had such a beautiful voice.

"Sarah left to go and play with the other children, for I could hear her voice trailing off into the distance. I had just picked up a large water jug to fill at the well. As I turned toward the door, a voice sounded in my ears, calling my name, 'Mary. Mary!' Startled, I turned to see who was calling. At first there was nothing to be seen, and then, a glow of soft light filled the room.

"Suddenly an angel of the Lord was standing before me. I was stunned and stood looking at him with utter amazement. He reached out and took the jug from my arms. His face was brilliant and his golden hair long and softly flowing. He was very much like the angels at the tomb. *Gabriel* was his name.

"I fell to my knees in reverence. When he spoke, a tremendous calm came over me. He announced these words: **'Hail, full of grace, the Lord is with thee: blessed art thou among women.'** (Luke 1:28)

"Confusion overwhelmed me at what he was saying. This was such a strange greeting.

'Do not be afraid, Mary, for you have found favor with God,' he continued. **'Fear not, Mary, for thou hast found grace with God. Behold thou shalt conceive in thy womb, and shalt bring** forth a son; and thou shalt call his name Jesus. He shall be great and shall be called the Son of the most High; and the Lord God shall give unto him the throne of David his father; and he shall reign in the house of Jacob for ever.' (Luke 1:30-33)

"You must realize that I was very young. I planned on remaining a virgin even though married, and, so, did not consider being a mother," Mary said to us. "My life had been dedicated as a Temple Virgin for the glory of the Father. In asking the angel how this could be, since I did not know man, he responded, **'The Holy Ghost shall come upon thee, and the power of the most High shall overshadow thee. And therefore also the Holy which shall be born of thee shall be called the Son of God.'** (Luke 1:35)

"My cousin Elizabeth, the mother of John, who was the Baptizer, was beyond the years of child bearing, but the angel further said, **'And behold thy cousin Elizabeth, she also hath conceived a son in her old age: and this is the sixth month with her that is called barren. Because no word shall be impossible with God.'** (Luke 1:36-37)

"I bowed my head in thought. I was betrothed to the carpenter Joseph and I wondered as to how he would accept such an announcement. My own parents would be the first to hear this news from my lips. The custom of our people is to stone a woman who is with child and not married. I think that for a moment a fear came over me. However, I have never refused God anything. The Law He has given, I have honored. How could I say no at this time? "The Messiah was to be born. The Father had asked me to be His spouse, through the power of His Spirit.

"Raising my head and looking at the angel, I said, **_'Behold the handmaid of the Lord: be it done to me according to thy word.'_** (Luke 1:38) After this the angel left.

"During my response to the angel, all fear of the unknown left me. Only one thing remained important and that was to do whatever the Father willed. Suddenly, surrounded by beautiful rays of light, colors of the rainbow swirled around me. It was the sign of the Holy Spirit. My white dress was spotted with golden dust and then, as quickly as it happened, all returned to normal. This sign

would happen many other times. My soul shall always be filled
with sublime joy for the fact that the Lord chose me, among all
women, to be the Mother of the Messiah. . . ."

These were very happy memories for her and she told them
with such humility. She continued her account of these early
memories and recalled her visit with the mother of John the
Baptizer.

"The angel gave me great news that my elderly cousin
Elizabeth was already in her sixth month and was to bear a son.
Poor Elizabeth had been barren and felt so inadequate. All those
years she and Zachariah constantly prayed for a child. Boy or girl-
it really never mattered. Once she was past her years, she was
accepting of the fact. However, there remained that spark of
hope."

Mary stopped for a moment, gazing up to Heaven, pondering
in heart and prayer, then continued.

"Zachariah was of the priestly class of Abijah. Elizabeth was
a descendent of Aaron. They were pleasing in the eyes and heart
of the Father. The Commandments and ordinances of the Lord
were written on their hearts, for they lived their lives in this fash-
ion, faithful and true.

"Within one day of the angel's announcement to me, I began
the journey to the town of Judah. The trip was tiring but my inner
energy source kept me going as fast as I possibly could. There
was no time to waste. They lived on the outskirts of town and
their house could easily be seen from a distance. "As I
approached along the narrow pathway, I could see Elizabeth
hanging the wash over the wooden racks Zachariah had made.

"I called out her name, and she looked up, quizzing herself as
to who was approaching. As her eyes focused on my face, she
began to smile and run toward me. It had been several years since
we last enjoyed time together.

"'Mary, my dear Mary! I rejoice in my Lord!' Elizabeth proclaimed. 'When I heard your greeting, the baby within me leapt
in my womb. The Holy Spirit has touched my soul and has given
me great wisdom. For blest are you among women and blest is the
fruit of your womb.' Bowing her head low, she humbled herself
and said, 'But who am I that the mother of my Lord should come

to me? The moment your greeting sounded in my ears, the baby leapt in my womb for pure joy. Blest is she who entrusted that the Lord's words to her would be fulfilled.'

"We embraced and cried, as we women do," she smiled and said. "Our tears were of amazement, of faith and trust, of joy in the word of the Lord. It was such a joyous moment, for such miraculous things were happening to both of us. The Holy Spirit enlightened my soul and I proclaimed:

> *My soul doth magnify the Lord*
> *And my spirit hath rejoiced in God my Saviour.*
> *Because he hath regarded the humility of his hand-*
> *maid: for behold from henceforth all generations*
>   *shall call me blessed.*
> *Because he that is mighty hath done great things to me:*
> *and holy is his name.*
> *And his mercy is from generation unto generations,*
> *to them that fear him.*
> *He hath shewed might in his arm:*
> *he hath scattered the proud in the conceit of their heart.*
> *He hath put down the mighty from their seat*
> *and hath exalted the humble.*
> *He hath filled the hungry with good things:*
> *and the rich he hath sent empty away.*
> *He hath received Israel his servant,*
> *being mindful of his mercy.*
> *As he spoke to our fathers:*
> *to Abraham and to his seed for ever.* (Luke 1:46-55)

"The three months I spent with Elizabeth and Zechariah were *very* special to all of us. We shared so much, for so much had happened. In between the normal needs of each day we recounted many things; especially, those things of the Lord's blessings upon us.

"Elizabeth told me of how it began: 'One day, while Zechariah was in the sanctuary of the Temple, offering incense unto the Lord, and the full assembly of people were praying outside at the hour of incense, an angel of the Lord appeared to him, standing at the right of the altar of incense. Zechariah was deeply disturbed upon seeing him and overcome by fear.

The angel said to him: *"Fear not, Zachary, for thy prayer is heard; and thy wife Elizabeth shall bear thee a son, and thou shalt call his name John. And thou shalt have joy and gladness; and many shall rejoice in his nativity. For he shall be great before the Lord; and shall drink no wine nor strong drink: and he shall be filled with the Holy Ghost, even from his mother's womb. And he shall convert many of the children of Israel to the Lord their God. And he shall go before him in the spirit and power of Elias: that he may turn the hearts of the fathers unto the children, and the incredulous to the wisdom of the just, to prepare unto the Lord a perfect people."* (Luke 1:13-17)

My husband responded, "How am I to know this? I am an old man; my wife, too, is beyond her child-bearing years."

Then angel Gabriel replied, **"I am Gabriel, who stand before God; and am sent to speak to thee, and to bring thee these good tidings. And behold, thou shalt be dumb, and shalt not be able to speak until the day wherein these things shall come to pass; because thou hast not believed my words, which shall be fulfilled in their time."** (Luke 1:19-20)

"'They were waiting for Zechariah, wondering at his delay. When he came out, he was unable to speak. They realized that he had seen a vision. He kept making signs to them, for he remained speechless.'"

Mary told of Elizabeth's desire to stay hidden for the first five months after her conception, choosing this time to stay in constant prayer with the Lord, to give praise and thanksgiving.

Eventually, Elizabeth delivered a fine, strong, healthy baby boy. The townspeople came to share in this miraculous event in their lives. They marveled that at her age this could happen. Only the power of God could have made it possible. The day was filled with jubilation.

Mary continued with her account of the birth of the Baptizer.

"On the eighth day after his birth, they assembled for the circumcision of the child, intending to call him after his father. When Elizabeth heard this, she stood up and stopped them and said, 'No, he is to be called *John*!'

"But they pointed out to her: 'None of your relatives have this name.'

"Then, using signs, they asked the father what he wished the child to be called. He signaled for a writing tablet and wrote the words, *'His name is John.'* This astonished them all. At that moment his mouth was opened and his speech returned. He began praising and thanking Almighty God.

"Over the next few weeks, the people recounted what had happened and it spread like wildfire. Some feared the news while others rejoiced that God was benefitting His people with His mercy. They wondered what kind of man this would be. Of this, we know. His destiny was to prepare the people for the Messiah and this he did."

I could not begin to write of all that Mother Mary told us but the following account of the Lord's birth was told in this way.

"After wandering around Bethlehem, trying to find a safe place to deliver the Baby, Joseph and I were taken to a cave where straw was strewn and various animals were kept. My immediate thought was one of sadness to think that my Baby, the Son of God, would be born in such a lowly place. Joseph, so wise, said, 'Jesus will be the Savior of all men and, therefore, as God among us, He will want to share in even the humblest of man's experience. God is the director of our lives, and if He wants His Son to be born here, among these, His creatures, should we not be content as if it were the palace itself?' His words gave great comfort. I knew he was right and joy flooded my soul.

"My time was at hand so Joseph went to seek the help of a midwife. It was really kind of funny because he had just walked out the door when the midwife met him. Esther said, 'You must be Joseph? I was sent to take care of your wife during the birthing. The Lord told me in a dream this night that I was to come here.'

"Joseph brought her in and she began fixing the hay and even directing Joseph to do this and that. Actually, this was good because like most men, he was becoming more and more nervous, the closer the time came. When things were ready, she had him sit on the straw next to me so he could give me comfort. "Poor Joseph," Mary recalled with a tender smile, "was trembling and then all of a sudden, he became relaxed and uttered a prayer. It was at that moment that a tremendous light of swirling colors engulfed us and we could hear angels singing hymns of praise. Soon we could hear the baby cry and all was back to its original state. Esther presented the baby to me. This little One had a special glow about Him. Joseph and I both looked at Him. Our hearts felt more love than we ever thought possible and we said, 'My Lord and My God!'

"As I held Him, He looked up at me and smiled. He reached out and held Joseph's finger. Esther was in tears and bowed her head, touching the ground saying, 'I have held Him who will save my children from their sins He who will bring peace to all people.'

"During the birth, a brilliant star showered down its light from up above. It's rays were so bright that they radiated light around the immediate area of perhaps a stone's throw in all directions. Joseph and Esther said that it was light as day where the star light struck. The townspeople came to see what was happening and there was a tremendous excitement on their faces.

"Shepherds came down from the hills and the outer areas of Bethlehem, exclaiming about the star and heavenly hosts of angels who exclaimed to them the great news of what had happened this night. Christ the Lord was born! People began gathering inside to see our Lord. Esther had taken Jesus and wrapped Him in swaddling clothes and laid Him in my arms again. Joseph returned to my side, and once again, Jesus took hold of his finger, clutching tightly and smiling so beautifully at him. Joseph had such a proud and happy smile on his face that he seemed to glow.

"Joseph always loved Jesus so much and kept a watchful eye on him. He protected us from all harm and adversity. I'm so grateful that he did not have to endure the Passion of Jesus. He sacrificed and worked very hard to provide for us. We loved him so much. How happy he must be to see how everything has turned out, the promise of the Father, fulfilled. "The shepherds brought many baby lambs as gifts but mostly you could see their presents were gifts of love. Many angels surrounded us, singing songs of praise, and some were swinging bowls of incense. The glory of the Lord shown around us, covering us with His pleasure.

"The townspeople prepared a celebration, a birthday party in honor of God's Son. There was dancing and singing and music played on string instruments. The air was filled with sounds of great joy, so melodious. Joseph and I raised our voices in song as Baby Jesus clapped His own tiny hands to the music."

We could picture these accounts as if they were happening right now. There were so many memories but one that she particularly liked to talk about was when He taught the teachers in the Temple.

"Jesus was only twelve years old, and like every year, we journeyed to Jerusalem to celebrate the feast of the Pasch. This was also a time for family and friends to gather together in a very holy and joyous way. Elizabeth, Zechariah and little John were there, and we spent a lot of time together. Zechariah recounted the time that we brought Jesus to the temple for Presentation."

Mary then recounted those memories for us.

"According to the Law of Moses, after Jesus was given the name commanded by the angel of the Lord, and received circumcision, we brought Him here to Jerusalem so that He could be rightly presented to the Lord. We bought two turtledoves to offer in sacrifice, according to the Law. When we went in to present Jesus in the Temple, an old man named Simeon came over to us. He was filled with joy and proclamation. He wanted to hold Jesus and Joseph was very skeptical at first. We both looked into his eyes and saw tears of real joy. He knew what we already knew, for God had revealed it to him. We found that He was just and pious and awaited the consolation of Israel. The Holy Spirit was upon him. It was revealed to him by the Holy Spirit that he would not experience death until he had seen the Anointed of the Lord. He came to the Temple that day, inspired by the Spirit, and so we handed Jesus to him to hold.

"As he raised his eyes heavenward, he proclaimed in a loud voice with tears running down his cheeks:

Now thou dost dismiss thy servant,
O Lord, according to thy word in peace:
Because my eyes have seen thy salvation,
Which thou hast prepared before the face of all peoples:
A light to the revelation of the Gentiles

and the glory of thy people Israel. (Luke 2:29-32)

"We were awestruck at what he was saying. Simeon then handed Jesus back to me. He looked up at me with a sadness on His little face as Simeon blessed us and further said, *'Behold this child is set for the fall, and for the resurrection of many in Israel, and for a sign which shall be contradicted; and thy own soul a sword shall pierce, that, out of many hearts, thoughts may be revealed.'* (Luke 2:34-35)

"Today, I fully understand those words he spoke. The little Baby in my arms also knew and His sadness was as if to say that He was sorry for what sorrow was destined to come."

Mary told us of the old woman, Anna, who came up to them and began preaching to all who waited for the Messiah that He was among them. Then, having fulfilled the prescription of the Law, they left for home.

She apologized for being sidetracked from the account she was beginning to tell. And then Barnabas asked, "Mother Mary, what happened at the Temple when Jesus was twelve. You said that you and Joseph found Jesus teaching the teachers."

"Yes!" Mary exclaimed. "We had gone to Jerusalem for the feast, and when it was over, we began the journey home. When everyone had gathered for the journey, Joseph and I noticed that Jesus was missing. But we were not concerned for surely He was with some of our relatives who would take good care of Him.

"By the end of the first day's journey, however, we checked with our relatives and found they thought He was with us. We were so afraid that something might have happened to Him. We hurried back to Jerusalem and searched all over the city for two days. We described Him to people but they would shout back, 'They all look alike,' or 'No, I've noticed no children.' It seemed that no one cared.

"Joseph was beside himself, heartsick, for he felt that he should have watched over Jesus more. We both had to share that responsibility. The thing that both of us forgot was the fact that God *was* watching over Him. Finally, we went to the Temple to pray and plead for God's assistance. As we bowed before the Lord, we heard the voice of Jesus very dimly. We looked at one another. We both had astonished faces. Joseph helped me to my feet, for my legs were somewhat shaky. We followed the direction of His voice into another section of the Temple and were astounded by what we saw.

"There, among the doctors of the Law, the teachers and other learned men, Jesus was *teaching* them. Rabbi Joachim ben Jacob posed Him a question: 'When the Israelites escaped the bondage of Egypt, God came to them in a pillar of cloud by day and a pillar of fire at night to protect them until they reached the promised land. What can you tell us of the pillar of fire?'

Jesus, in all quickness and assurance, responded, as the Creator of all powerful light, God can use all kinds of light to manifest His Presence, and the pillar was the miraculous, visible manifestation of the Divine Presence, but His glory was veiled. This pillar, which cannot be understood, had the appearance of smoke by day and would shelter the people from the heat of the sun, and the appearance of fire by night. So, the people had no darkness at all. Thus, it guarded as well as guided them. Fire also symbolizes God's purity and glory.

"The Rabbi, in shock of the brilliant Boy before him, sat down with great force. All those assembled for this session were in great amazement at each and every question posed and answered by Jesus. Yes, Joseph and I were also amazed by the wonders He performed. Perplexed by the whole incident, I gently walked over to Him and asked why He did not leave with us. His answer was so simple: *'How is it that you sought me? did you not know, that I must be about my father's business?'* (Luke 2:49)

"In my heart I knew that the day would come when He would do just that. But for now, God gave him to us to nurture and teach- although teaching was something that He could do for us.

"Jesus was a very good and devoted Son. He loved working with Joseph and when He was only five, He built His first chair. If Joseph had a project that he could not finish because of an errand away, Jesus had it finished when he came home. He always asked what He could do to help me around the house. When I went to the well for water, He would run after me and carry it back. I was always very proud of him."

At times Mary's voice would become very low and her eyes would begin to close. She needed to rest so Joanna and Claudia escorted her to another area where she could rest quietly. As they walked away, Mary turned, her eyes searching for something. When they came to rest on me, she said, "I'm so glad you are here. We love you very much. In the cabinet behind you, you will find something wrapped in brown linen; you will cherish it for its worth." Then she turned and followed the other two.

Later I went over to the cabinet. I took up the linen packet, unwrapped it and found one of the nails that had pierced my Master's hands and feet. Cherished shall it be, a relic of faith in the One Who loves us so much that He opened wide His arms to show us *how much* as they nailed them to the cross.

Unlike the rest of us, Mary spent a lot of time talking to people near the Temple. She never seemed to fear anything. She told us that "since Jesus has risen as He promised, He has destroyed fear. If we live in Him, nothing can truly harm us." She was really the first missionary. All the responsibilities that she took upon her self was truly exemplary. "You have become the family of Jesus, and as His mother, He has, through His love, made me your mother. I will care for you as I did for Him," she said often.

From the time Jesus resurrected from the tomb until His Ascension, He spent forty days on earth. Our Lord let Himself be seen by all of us on a number of occasions. Two of His Disciples, Ephraim and Malchus, had met Him on the way to Emmaus. They hurried back at once to Simeon's house. Here in Jerusalem they excitedly recounted their experience.

"We walked and talked with Him for miles and had no idea it was Him. But when we sat to eat, our eyes were opened. As we were gathered together, our Lord came, showed us the wounds in His hands and feet. Then He broke and gave us the bread and poured the wine, bidding us to drink. Our eyes filled with tears and our hearts were ready to burst with the pure love with which He fed us. We begged Him to stay the night with us as it was getting dark. But the Lord had others to see and places to go."

Eight days after the meeting with Ephraim and Malchus, Jesus returned to us, who were gathered in the upper room. This time Thomas was also present. He had missed the other appearances and stubbornly could not accept that Jesus had risen as He promised. He even doubted Mother Mary, telling her, "Dearest

Mary, you have lost your Son and we have lost our truest Friend. In your sorrow you want so much to believe. I'm so sorry for you in your pain. I just can't bring myself to believe."

Mary just said, "You will see Him soon, and you, too, will believe for He will bring you to it. Your heavy doubt will be put to rest, my son. Although, you will probably be known as 'Thomas Who Doubts.'" She said this jokingly and the others kidded him.

Peter then spoke up: "How can you doubt us; especially, this woman, His own mother, she who has been given to us as our own mother? We, your brothers, have eaten and drunk with Him several times. Jesus Himself told us that He would rise on the third day. Do you even doubt Him?"

Thomas retorted, "Unless I myself put my own fingers into His wounds and place my hand into His side, I will not believe." He was stubborn but wanting to believe. He broke down in a flood of tears over his lack of faith.

This day, however, he was with us, and we were preparing to eat. The doors, as usual, were locked. Thomas was looking out the window, down into the street. Suddenly, behind him stood the Lord Jesus. He greeted us, saying, *"Peace be to you."* (John 20:19) Thomas spun around, recognizing the voice of the Master. His eyes were wide and his mouth dropped open. Then Jesus looked at Thomas and spoke, *"Put in thy finger hither and see my hands; and bring hither thy hand, and put it into my side; and be not faithless, but believing."* (John 20:27)

Thomas fell to his knees and bowing low responded, *"My Lord and my God!"* (John 20:28)

Addressing not only Thomas, but all of us, Jesus said, *"Because thou hast seen me, Thomas, thou hast believed: blessed are they that have not seen and have believed."* (John 20:29)

Later, the Apostles left Jerusalem and went into Galilee in accordance with the Master's instructions. One evening Peter, with six other Apostles, set out to fish in the lake. All night they fished but caught nothing. At dawn they saw a stranger on the shore and when they had pulled near, this man told them to cast their net on the other side of the boat. They did so. Immediately, they made such a catch that they could not raise the net. In that instant, Peter recognized Him and cried out, "It is the Lord!" He then jumped into the water, and, with his usual quickness, swam the hundred yards to the shore.

It was a joyful reunion. At His invitation, they built a fire and prepared a meal. Then they settled down to hear the Master's words. He took the occasion to confirm Peter as our leader and continued the training for the commission He gave them: *"Going therefore, teach ye all nations: baptizing them in the name of the Father, and of the Son, and of the Holy Ghost. . . ."* (Matt. 28:19)

At an appointed time, our Lord's devoted followers went to Jerusalem and were met there by Jesus. It was then that He imparted to us His final instructions. His teaching would announce repentance and forgiveness of sin. It would be for all nations and would begin in Jerusalem.

When His last words were uttered, Jesus Christ, true God and true Man, whose birth was a miracle, left the earth in a miraculous way. With His mother, the Apostles, Disciples and holy women gathered around Him on Mount Olivet, He bid us farewell. As He blessed us, a mighty light surrounded Him, radiating rays of beautiful and varied hues of gold, red, green and blue. A brilliant white cloud surrounded His feet, and slowly, He was lifted up.

During His ascent into Heaven, the eyes of mother and Son continued to gaze into each other. Mary's own face glowed magnificently with a reflection of Christ's own glory. Their eyes spoke of undying love. There was no sadness or goodbye in their faces.

As we gazed up to Heaven, two men in dazzling white tunics suddenly stood beside us. With angelic voices they asked, *"Ye men of Galilee, why stand you looking up to heaven? This Jesus who is taken up from you into heaven, shall so come as you have seen him going into heaven."* (Acts 1:11)

It remained quiet for several minutes. All of us felt such peace and tranquility. Matthew broke the silence: "The Lord has been lifted up and we shall miss Him. He was the greatest of all teachers, truly our Messiah, but how will we live without Him?"

As she rose to her feet, Mary spoke to all of us in a voice of assurance: "My Son has not left us. He told us He will be with us, even to the end of the world. In a few days Jesus will send us His Mighty Spirit, just as the Father sent Him to me on the day Angel Gabriel first visited me so many years ago. We are not orphans who are lost with no one to care for them. We are a family that the Father in Heaven has gathered together. For all ages to come, the Lord will bless us and direct us. By His Spirit He will continue to guide us, to direct us on our pathway. We will never be alone."

Our Holy Mother continued, "Each time we share in the Breaking of the Bread, He is alive in our presence. John, when you and the others take the Holiest of Bread, His very Body and Blood, to our brethren who are invalids, you carry Him in your arms as I carried Him as a Baby. No, He has not left us but will soon give us all that we need to do the work He has given us to do. Soon, very soon, your strength and faith will increase a thousand times, and through the power of the Holy Spirit, you will do things in His Name, beyond your imaginations. Didn't Jesus just tell us to wait for *'for the promise of the Father, which you have heard (saith he) by my mouth. For John indeed baptized with water; but you shall be baptized with the Holy Ghost.'* (Acts 1:4-5) She continued, "Jesus said that you will receive power when the Holy Spirit comes down on you; then you are to be His witnesses in Jerusalem, throughout Judea and Samaria, even to the ends of the earth."

Mary turned, looked up in the direction Jesus ascended and prayed, "My Lord and My God, My Son and My Savior, I will serve You all my days. My will is Yours. I will care for all those You have given me. I will love them with an undying love. For all times I will be your humble servant and lead them to You."

Mary kept us on our toes with her motherly guidance. We are so fortunate to have her always with us.

Peter rose from where he was kneeling and said, "Let us return to Jerusalem, where we shall await the Holy Spirit." Our travel was quick, so it seemed, as we pondered on all that had happened.

Many of us stayed in the upper room of Simeon's house: the eleven Apostles, the mother of Jesus and their family, many holy women and several men, all devoted to Jesus. We spent our days in constant prayer and praise. In estimate, we numbered about one hundred and fifty. Mary and the other women took care of the tasks of the house and meals, as usual. To see Mary in her relations with the other women, while concerned with these tasks, would make any man envious of having such a task master-so kind to everyone and first to do the heaviest of tasks. One day Mirianna had been scrubbing the floor. She seemed so very tired that Mary went over to her and asked her if she would like to rest. Mirianna refused to rest and so Mary left and returned with a duplicate set of things with which to clean. She knelt, looked at Mirianna and said, "Now, it will be done in half the time and then we can both rest."

However, she always found something else to do. Everything she did was done as if it were a prayer. Each task was for ". . .the glory of God." Besides these household tasks, she spent many hours in prayer and prayed or sang all the Psalms each day.

One day while we were in community prayer, Peter stood up and addressed us most earnestly: ***"Men, brethren, the scripture must needs be fulfilled, which the Holy Ghost spoke before by the mouth of David concerning Judas, who was the leader of them that apprehended Jesus: Who was numbered with us, and had obtained part of this ministry.***

"And he indeed hath possessed a field of the reward of iniquity, and being hanged, burst asunder in the midst: and all his bowels gushed out. And it became known to all the inhabitants of Jerusalem: so that the same field was called in their tongue, Haceldama, that is to say, The field of blood.

> ***For it is written in the book of Psalms:***
> ***Let their habitation become desolate,***
> ***and let there be none to dwell therein.***
> ***And his bishopric let another take.***

Wherefore of these men who have companied with us all the time that the Lord Jesus came in and went out among us. Beginning from the baptism of John, until the day wherein he was taken up from us, one of these must be made a witness with us of his resurrection." (Acts 1:16-22)

John spoke up and gave a name in nomination: "A good and devout man, a true friend and Disciple of Our Lord from almost the beginning, I wish to nominate Matthias." Andrew nominated another called Barsabbas. With these two nominations, all that were assembled, about one hundred fifty, began to pray.

Jude Thaddeus stood to lead the prayer: *"Thou, Lord, who knowest the hearts of all men, shew whether of these two thou hast chosen, to take the place of this ministry and apostleship, from which Judas hath by transgression fallen, that he might go to his own place."* (Acts 1:24-25)

The eleven each took two colored stones, one black and one red, and according to his choice, dropped one into a basket. Barsabbas was black and Matthias was red. When the stones were tallied, Matthias had been elected.

Matthias was welcomed and greeted by the whole assembly. Our Mother Mary embraced him and proclaimed, "The Holy Spirit has anointed you worthy." Then Peter and the others who were Apostles, laid hands on him in prayer that he might be officially anointed through the Holy Spirit. With Holy Oil they did anoint his hands and head. There was a festival this day, for a brother was lost and a new brother given.

The time was drawing near when the Holy Spirit would descend upon us. Even the women began to be more earnest in their prayers. Some of the household tasks would have to wait, although few of them did.

CHAPTER 4

Come, Holy Spirit, Come

Cyrene

My dear cousin Jacob,

Please greet Marcellus as you would me, for he comes to you in my place. I pray that this letter which he bears has been delivered safely. Marcellus has been my friend, confident and companion now for the past six years, traveling and bearing witness to the truth. Please give him shelter and protection.

I know that you have not shared in this truth of Jesus Christ, but in my death I pray that you will come to see the light.

It has been nearly six years since that day when I first entered Jerusalem to visit friends. That wonderful, yet very sad day, when I met my Lord and Savior, Jesus Christ for the first time. So much has happened since that day. Now I sit here in my cell, waiting for my sentence to be carried out.

If I could go back in time, I would change nothing. Life would be a burden if it were not for the great joy that Jesus has afforded me. Oh, if only you could know that joy, that peace!

Along with this letter, I entrust to you my simple journal. Much of my writing has been lost over these past few years, but in the time yet allowed me, I will hurriedly scribble some of those memories. A guard has promised to deliver this to Marcellus, who in turn will bring them to you. (From Simon's final letter to his cousin Jacob)

After the Lord ascended to the Father, those of us who went with Him to Mount Olivet, returned to Jerusalem and the home of Simeon. Here we awaited the Holy Spirit, whom the Lord promised to send. Our days were spent in prayer and fasting, as well as recounting the things of which the Lord spoke to us. The women, while keeping prayer vigil, found time to take care of everyday needs and to see that nothing was lacking.

It was on the day of the Feast of Weeks, Pentecost, when the Holy Spirit came upon us. At about eight in the morning we were resting and quietly talking. Mother Mary and the women had finished tidying up after the meal. Barsabbas had just come in with fresh water from the well. Joanna, Claudia and Martha were preparing to spin some wool. Peter had just uttered a prayer: "Come, Holy Spirit, Come! Illuminate us with Your Counsel."

Suddenly, there was a loud noise coming from the heavens like great gusts of strong wind. Yet, there was no wind, only a gentle breeze. Some of us placed our hands over our ears or our prayer shawls over our heads.

Then we saw the manifestation of the Holy Spirit! The room was thick with magnificent rays of colors and sparkles of gold, swirling around us, enveloping us in a loving and tender embrace. Then, upon the head of each one in that room-man, woman and child alike-a glow, like a tongue of fire, settled. It did not injure or burn us in any way.

As for myself, I began to see clearly, more clearly than ever before. I felt a burning deep within my soul; joy, as I had never felt before. Things that I had not as yet learned or understood about Jesus, I suddenly knew and comprehended, as if I had walked with Him all my life. I wanted to shout out to the whole world about Jesus, my Savior!

We ran down the stairs and into the street, calling out our praises to God and His Son, proclaiming the great news of our deliverance in Christ. We proclaimed to all who could hear us.

Matthew shouted out: "If you have ears that hear, *listen!* Ears that are closed shall be opened! Mouths that have been silent will shout aloud their joy and proclaim the goodness of the Lord! Hearts of stone will become like bread put to soak in the glory of the Risen Lord!"

Once we asked the Lord if He was going to restore the kingdom of Israel. To this He responded, ***"It is not for you to know the time or moments, which the Father hath put in his own power: But you shall receive the power of the Holy Ghost com-***

ing upon you, and you shall be witnesses unto me in Jerusalem, and in all Judea, and Samaria, and even to the uttermost part of the earth." (Acts 1:7-8) This He said before He was transfigured in glory. This day we saw His words being fulfilled.

Jerusalem was very crowded during this great feast and people had come from many nations. They who had heard the loud noise began gathering into groups, quizzing each other as to what this noise meant.

When we burst forth into the street they became even more confused, astonished, even awe struck at what they heard. Confusion ran rampant because those assembled could hear the words proclaimed in their own tongues! The crowd questioned one another: "Aren't these men who are speaking *Galilean*?"

"How is it that each of us hears them in his own native tongue?"

"We are Parthians and Medes."

"I and my household are from Mesopotamia, and like you, we know his words!"

"We are a mixed crowd from all over the world: Judea, Cappadocia, Pontus and Asia."

People from all parts of the world heard us. Egyptians, those from Libya and our own people from Cyrene were present. Ishmael, our kinsman, shouted out that we were all drunk on cheap wine. But that could not explain what was happening.

Peter stood up with the Eleven, lifted his voice above the murmurings and shouts and addressed the gathering: "Fellow Jews! All of you who live in Jerusalem! Let me explain! Listen carefully to what I say.

"These men are not drunk! It's only nine in the morning! No! Why, the prophet Joel spoke of this:

> *'And it shall come to pass, in the last days,*
> *(saith the Lord),*
> *I will pour out of my Spirit upon all flesh:*
> *and your sons and your daughters shall prophesy,*
> *and your young men shall see visions,*
> *and your old men shall dream dreams.*

And upon my servants indeed and upon my handmaids
will I pour out in those days of my spirit,
and they shall prophesy.
And I will shew wonders in the heaven above,
and signs on the earth beneath:
blood and fire, and vapour of smoke.
The sun shall be turned into darkness,
and the moon into blood,
before the great and
manifest day of the Lord come.
And it shalt come to pass, that whosoever
shall call upon the name of the Lord
shall be saved.' (Acts: 17-21)

"Listen to me! Jesus of Nazareth was a man accredited by God to you by miracles and great wonders and signs. God worked these through Him!" I wondered for a moment about those who would come many years after us. Would they continue in their Faith? We have seen with our own eyes, experienced with our very beings these glories. Would the day come when followers of His would deny Him, more so than Peter, or even Judas the betrayer?

Peter continued, "This Man was handed over to you by God according to His own plan. But you, you put Him to death! You nailed Him to a cross!   "Yet God raised Him from the dead, freeing Him because it was impossible for death to keep hold of Him.

"Why, our father, David, once said about Him:

I foresaw the Lord before my face:
because he is at my right hand,
that I may not be moved.
For this my heart hath been glad,
and my tongue hath rejoiced:
moreover my flesh also shall rest in hope.
Because thou wilt not leave my soul in hell,
nor suffer thy Holy One to see corruption.
Thou hast made known to me the ways of life:
thou shalt make me full of joy with thy
countenance. (Acts 2:25-28)

"Brothers, I tell you with great confidence that the patriarch David died, was buried. His tomb is here to this very day. But he was a prophet! He knew that God had vowed to one day place his descendant on his throne. As a prophet, he spoke of the future. He spoke of the Resurrection of the Christ! Christ was not abandoned to the grave! Christ's body did not decay. God raised Christ to life! We are all witnesses!"

Peter's excitement could not be contained:

> *"Being exalted therefore by the right hand of God,*
> *and having received of the Father*
> *the promise of the Holy Ghost,*
> *he hath poured forth this which you see and hear."*
> (Acts 2:33)

"David did not ascend to Heaven, but he did say:

> *'The Lord said to my Lord,*
> *"Sit thou on my right hand,*
> *until I make thy enemies thy footstool.'*
> (Acts 2:34-35)

"Oh my dear brothers and sisters, let all Israel know this as true: God has made this Jesus - the One whom you crucified-both Lord and Christ!"

It was amazing how this multitude of people fell silent in order to hear Peter. Many had tears in their eyes and their faces bore the signs of great remorse. For many of these same people, just weeks ago, had shouted, "Crucify him! Crucify Him!" Many began to clutch their chests and plead, "Brothers, what must we do?" I knew the feeling of that great desire to know more and to become a true follower.

Peter began speaking again: "Repent! Be baptized, every one of you, in the name of Jesus Christ. Your sins will be forgiven and you will receive the Gift of the Holy Spirit! The promise is for you! For your children! For all who are far off! For all whom the Lord our God will call."

Peter spoke for sometime, and all listened attentively to his words-words that came forth from the very Spirit of God. "Save yourselves from this corrupt generation."

I don't know exactly how many were there listening and being transformed in spirit. I believe that there must have been at least 3,000 baptized and thus counted among the servants of the

Lord. The Apostles laid hands upon them and they were filled with the Holy Spirit of God.

This was a very busy day for all of us. We, who had been in the Upper Room and experienced the great Descent, were busy baptizing and teaching. No question was impossible to answer confidently. It was the Holy Spirit who spoke through us. He gave us the utterance and the wisdom. He gave us all the knowledge we needed in order to respond.

People began sitting down in groups, each with an Apostle or Disciple of the Lord. Many of the women went to sit at our Holy Mother's feet to learn more and to be edified. Her face glowed with a special radiance. Many of the holy women gathered the children among them and the children, too, were edified.

I recall now my own *personal* experience of the Holy Spirit's descent upon us in the Upper Room. As the Holy Spirit overwhelmed us with His mighty blessings and powerful gifts, we swooned into a peaceful state of great joy. The feeling that came over me was one of confidence, strength, endurance, assurance and an uplifting of body and spirit! An awesome serenity flooded my being.

In remembering the day I first received the Lord in the form of Bread and Wine, a deeper sense of humility took hold of my soul, for it was then that I first became attuned to this newness of life. I realized that there was a fullness, a sort of completion that had been unknown to me. It felt as though thousands upon thousands of grains of sand rushed through my whole being from head to toe. It was a surge of energy that man has never felt before. Of this I was certain!

However, when I looked at Mother Mary, I realized that she had experienced something similar before. She was not a stranger to the workings of the Holy Spirit. She was sitting in a chair by the wall. Her face glowed with a radiance of light that was almost blinding; yet, so easy to look at. Her face, uplifted toward the heavens, was utterly peaceful. Her lips moved softly in prayer. Her whole body was an expression of total ecstasy.

On her lap, her hands rested, palms up in a receiving gesture. Was she gazing upon her Spouse, the Holy Spirit? Was she being given graces that will last throughout eternity? Was she learning the fullness of her mission and accepting it as she did many years ago when the Angel Gabriel came to her?

All of us gathered in the Upper Room that day shared these awesome beginnings. I use the word *beginnings* because this day was the real start of the ministry for which Jesus had prepared His Apostles. This was the day that those of us chosen to be present would begin a deeper service to our brothers and sisters in Jesus Christ. This was the birthday of the Messiah's Church.

He was the *new Temple* that would be destroyed, but three days later, rebuilt. *He* was horribly crucified and death took Him. *He* was laid in a tomb, and in three days rose, body and soul, never more to die.

I am witness to these events. I have seen the Lord, in person, since His rising. You may think me a foolish man, but by all that is holy, I attest to its validity. Yes! Even to my very death, which soon awaits my body, but not my soul.

That truly was a day to remember, and the following days were just as fantastic. In fact, each day since has been truly a rewarding and blessed event. Although I am locked up behind these walls, hearing the horrid stories of what awaits as my execution comes closer, I am *free*! I've never felt more alive since the day when I first took up His cross and placed it upon my own shoulders; when I felt His blood from the cross upon my hands; when our eyes met and no word was needed to express what was felt and understood.

CHAPTER 5

Alexander And Rufus

Did you know, dearest Jacob, that your cousins, my sons, Alexander and Rufus, both came to know the Lord? It was about eight weeks after Pentecost that we finally met again. It had been nearly two years since I last saw them. Cousin Ishmael was the one who told them where I could be found. We were no longer in hiding. (From Simon's final letter to his cousin Jacob)

I walked with John, the Beloved Disciple, and Mother Mary in the Garden of Gethsemane, the place where Jesus loved to pray. We sat for a moment to rest and to reflect. John asked me if I had seen my two sons yet. He mentioned that they were in Jerusalem and wanted to see me. My heart leapt for joy at the thought of a reunion.

Mary smiled, saying, "Oh, Simon, what joy it will be for you and your sons to meet after so long. We shall keep this meeting in our prayers."

"Mary," I told her, "I don't know how they will receive me and my new found faith. Rufus, the younger, was going to study under Rabbi Benjamin to become a rabbi. Alexander has been somewhat of a scoundrel, living life 'to the fullest.' In spite of their differences, however, both boys have remained close. "Their mother died when they were still youths. Alexander was fourteen and Rufus, twelve. Alexander was away from the village when Jolema passed on, so he never saw her in the last days of her illness. He was busy with his friends, who were so important to him. Perhaps it was his age.

"Rufus, on the other hand, attended his mother day and night. Many times we had to tell him to go to bed at night and take his rest. When I had to be away, even for a few minutes, Rufus was

53

right there. On the day Jolema died, Rufus was reciting the Psalms of David. She so loved his recitations.

"After just coming in from the morning's errands, I sat in a chair across the room from where she lay. Rufus was sitting by her side and had just begun David's Twenty-Third Psalm:

The Lord ruleth me:
  and I shall want nothing.
He hath set me in a place of pasture.
He hath brought me up, on the water of refreshment:
he hath converted my soul.
He hath led me on the paths of justice,
for his own name's sake.
For though I should walk in the midst of
  the shadow of death,
I will fear no evils, for thou art with me.
Thy rod and thy staff, they have comforted me.
(Psalm 22:1-4)

"At that point, she placed her hands over his heart and asked him: 'Rufus, my son, what will become of you? Your heart beats with great love for Him Who Is Merciful. You have so much to give for the sake of all. You love the Law of God and you follow His commands. You, my darling son, should be a teacher of God's Law, a rabbi.'

"Rufus answered her, 'Oh Mother, this has been in my heart. If Father will agree, then I shall follow this path.'

"Of course I accepted, and when he was in his fourteenth year, he began studies under the tutorial guidance of Rabbi Benjamin. Alexander returned home in time for Jolema's burial. At the burial he promised his mother that he would watch over his brother and care for him. Of course he had other things in his life that seemed so much more important, but he and his brother became closer than they had been in their early years. This closeness continued to grow throughout the years and eventually they became good companions for each other. However, when Alexander wanted to be wild with his friends, he and Rufus would part ways for short periods of time.

"Once Rufus fell and broke his leg. When Alexander heard about it, he left his friends and rushed to his assistance. They are good boys. Rufus did not become a rabbi but he lives a very holy life in obedience to God."

I stopped my reminiscing and Mother Mary smiled at me. "Simon," she said, "tomorrow, please come to our house. And bring your sons. John and I will welcome them as our own."

John smiled, nodding his own acceptance. He said, "I wanted this to be a surprise for you but Ishmael is bringing Alexander and Rufus to you tonight. Did you know that Ishmael was baptized this morning?" He grinned as he continued, "He has found the Lord and he now knows for certain that we were *not* drunk on Pentecost."

I could hardly believe my ears, although in my heart I had known that the Lord would touch him.

That evening, shortly before sunset, Ishmael, Alexander and Rufus arrived. It was a celebration of great joy. We embraced one another, declaring our love.

They looked strong and healthy. Alexander was big and muscular-no doubt from having to defend himself and not just a few times! Rufus was still the mild one with serenity radiating from within.

In the midst of the confusion, I failed to see the others who were with them. Two very attractive young women with shy smiles were waiting to be introduced. Alexander and Rufus had both taken wives. Rufus had married Rachel, and Alexander, Naomi.

There was yet another member of the family waiting to meet me. It was little Joshua, Rufus' son, not quite a year old. Then to my happy surprise, Alexander told me that Naomi was with child. "If it is a girl, we are going to name her Jolema after mother, and if it is a boy, Simon, after you. Tears welled up in my eyes and my heart filled with such tenderness. We were a family. But there was still more for me to discover the next day when we went to the home of Mary and John.

That night we all found room for sleeping, even with all the others who stayed there. You see, although Simeon's Upper Room had been used for the Lord's Last Supper, it became the home of many from then on. It was a shelter, a refuge for all who were in need during those early days.

My family met all the Apostles and Disciples. Mother Mary expressed her delight that they would share a meal in her home the following day. My family soon relaxed, becoming totally at ease with all present.

The next day we shared news of what had taken place since last we were together. Rufus had much to tell but was holding back something in excitement. I didn't pressure him for it because there was so much to catch up on. This was the first time that John and Mother Mary had not come by the house. They must have been very busy preparing for the anticipated meal.

Andrew came over to Rachel and lifted up little Joshua, declaring, "This little one, a special child of the Lord, will one day see many blessed in Christ. His little hand will extend to many."

Rachel looked at me and tears came to her eyes. Andrew then handed her baby back to her and she smiled contentedly while embracing Joshua. Rufus caught the quizzical look on my face and began to talk about other things. James, the brother of John, approached and asked my sons to accompany him on an errand. They were gone for some time, and upon their return, it was time to leave for the home of Mary and John.

It was about a thirty-minute walk and the streets of Jerusalem were crowded. Along the way several people acknowledged us as we passed. They were friends who knew us and were blessed in the Lord Jesus. One, a women known as Philomena, stopped us to inquire about my family. Many of our friends already knew that they were in the city, for word had spread quickly. It was strange how my sons and their wives seemed to fit right in as if they had always belonged. This was exciting for me because my prayer was that they would accept Christ as their own Lord and Savior.

At the home of Mary and John, we were received with open arms and the special greeting in Jesus. At first I feared that my sons might react negatively to the friends of Jesus, but to my joy, it was just the opposite.

We sat down at table and Mary brought in a special meal. She served lamb and vegetables with fresh baked bread. John placed a decanter of wine on the table, as well as a pitcher of water. After thanking God for all His many blessings, I offered this additional prayer: "Lord, Jesus Christ, I thank you for bringing my family back into my life, and for Your many blessings, known and unknown. Ask our Father in Heaven to guide Alexander, Rufus and their wives unto Your promise. Look upon Joshua and hold him in the palm of Your hand."

We ate. The conversation was good and following the meal, we praised God. Naomi and Rachel helped Mary clear the table while the men sat talking about the mercy of God. I was surprised that Alexander spoke so well on this topic. Perhaps Rufus had more effect on him than I had once thought.

Not long after, there was a knock on the door. Peter had arrived with the other Apostles. Matthias, the newest member, went into the kitchen to speak with the women. Alexander and Rufus went over to Peter and James to speak privately. The rest of us enlarged our circle, and after greeting one another, joined in conversation about the Lord.

When Matthias and the women returned, Rachel spoke, startling me with her news. "Peter, tonight is the night that I am filled with great joy. You have prepared, through Jesus our Lord, a blessing that will be forever upon my family and all my descendants."

What was she saying? Did Rachel know Peter? Of what blessing was she speaking?

Then Naomi also spoke up and said, "And in my house the Lord has given a blessing. He has blessed us with the child that is to be born into our lives. But our greatest blessing is that we have found the Lord, Jesus Christ, and it is He that we shall always serve."

This was too much! I was certain that my heart would burst with pure joy! And then Peter spoke, "My sisters, Naomi and Rachel, it is the joy of the House of Jesus Christ, of whom we are all brothers and sisters."

As tears rolled down my face and gathered in the curls of my beard, Peter looked at me and said, "And to you, our dear brother, whom the Lord has blessed so many times, even from the moment you held His cross, He gives even more. For today your joy will be complete. You see, we have known Alexander and

Rufus since the day of the Fish and the Loaves. You know, the day
the Lord fed five thousand with only five loaves of bread and two
fish."

Then James spoke up: "The Lord asked us to request that the
multitude be seated on the ground. There were so many gathered
to hear the Master. Under a nearby tree sat two men who were
very attentive to the Lord's teaching. We were to meet them later
after all had been fed."

Alexander explained, "We were close enough to hear and see
what this Rabbi was doing. Our reason for going was pure curios-
ity. But what we beheld was a new purpose-a direction to our lives
that would carry us through for all eternity.

"You know how I lived, Father, always the prankster, never
caring about who I hurt. I was shameful and I dishonored you and
the memory of my mother. But when I heard Jesus speak, I really
listened-not just with my ears but with my heart. Rufus and I witnessed the miracle of the Fish and Loaves. We ate until we were
filled, as did all the others. There must have been eight thousand
or more, including women and children. Yet, there were twelve
over-flowing baskets remaining. I know because Rufus and I
helped gather these crumbs. This was not some cheap magic trick
but the very hand of God, feeding His people with next to nothing.

"After we ate and helped collect the left overs, Rufus and I
asked to speak to the Lord. Judas wanted us to go away but Philip
interceded for us and Jesus received us. We vowed then that we
would follow the Master."

"We did follow Him," Rufus spoke up, "and then one day He
told us that in our family we would be greatly blessed in serving
God. I asked him if we could go to Cyrene and speak to our father
and kinsman about Him. He smiled and said, 'Be on your way.'
Then He prayed a blessing over us.

"We went home, but we could not find you, Father. We stayed
and prayed that you would return soon. Meanwhile, we spoke to
our kinsmen about the teachings of Christ. Eventually, when we
heard that the Lord had been arrested, we returned to Jerusalem.
By the time we arrived, the Lord was hanging on the cross and a
spear had pierced His side.

"Alexander and I helped take down His body and lay Him in the newly cut tomb of Joseph of Arimathea. As the Lord's body was being slowly lowered by ropes from the cross, His mother waited there with John to receive Him. Both reached up and Alexander and I hurried to their side. Mary went to her knees from pure weakness, and then sitting upon the ground, received and held her Son's lifeless body. As she held Him, she kissed His blood- covered face and hands, staining her own hands and face with His blood. At first she could not speak and her chest rose and fell rapidly. Finally, a deep sorrowful scream broke loose from deep within her, and bitter, painful sounds rent the air. Her tears fell so heavily that they washed His blood from her face.

"From that moment we stayed with the others until after the Resurrection. Then we went back to Cyrene to find you. How funny that you were here all along. But now, praise the Lord, we are together again."

As I listened to my sons, I recognized their special role in the Eternal Father's Plan. God directs our lives if we allow Him. He speaks to us and He guides us in ways that we don't always see. All we need to do is keep our hearts open to His call. Speak Lord, Your servant is listening. I come to do Your Will.

This was such a joyous occasion for me. My sons and their families would live forever in the Lord Jesus. Peter said to me, "Simon, this night, you will have the joy of bearing witness to the baptism of your family in the Lord. They will become, by pre-scription of the Faith, by profession of the very Blood of Jesus, true members of the family of Christ. This night they will be bap-tized by water and fire. The fire of the Holy Spirit will come upon them and their spirits shall be lifted up. They shall be counted among the saints, the chosen ones."

James had returned from somewhere outside and informed us that all was ready. He had gone to make sure that it was safe to go to the stream to carry out the ritual. Although we were open about our new Faith, we still had need of some precaution. The author-ities were looking for ways to silence us and wipe out all memo-ry of the very name of Jesus.

Matthias thought that it might be wiser to go in little groups to the stream so as not to draw suspicion upon us. We agreed and left in groups of three and four. There were at least three different ways to get to the stream so the different groups left in different directions.

Upon reaching the stream, we waited for all to gather. The only light we had was the light that God provided, that of the moon and the stars. Moon light reflected upon the water where Peter and James stood, waiting to baptize my sons, their wives and little Joshua.

"Almighty Father," began Peter, "Your children are gathered here to bring forth Your servants to be baptized in You and made brothers and sisters of the Lord Jesus Christ. We ask You to set Your light in them, the light of Your Holy Spirit, and give them the gifts that only You can bestow. Let them be the extension of Your Son Jesus Christ into this nation and every nation. Amen."

After lowering his hands, James called Alexander and Naomi to come forward. Rufus, Rachel and Joshua were called forth by Peter. I moved closer to hear and witness this solemn occasion, remembering my own rebirth at the river. All of a sudden, I heard other names being called farther off, and I realized that the other Apostles were also in the water, baptizing. Praise be to the Son of God, Our Lord Jesus Christ!

During these days, those who heard the call of Jesus and were baptized were living in common wherever they could. Many of the wealthy and not- so-wealthy sold what they had and distributed the alms according to the needs of the community.

Many miracles were done. The Apostles walked with great authority from the Lord, healing the blind, giving sound to the deaf, making the lame walk, and working such wonders in the name of Jesus that many came to believe. Meals were shared in common, and afterward, they would break bread as one or another of the Apostles presided at prayer. Every day the Lord continued to add to His number of faithful.

One day when Peter and John were going to the Temple at the three o'clock hour, a man crippled from birth was being brought in on a stretcher. This was normal for him as this is where he begged for alms from passersby. But on this particular day, Peter spoke up, saying, *"Look upon us . . . Silver and gold I have none; but what I have, I give thee: In the name of Jesus Christ of Nazareth, arise and walk.."* (Acts 3:4, 6) As he took him by the right arm, Peter pulled the beggar up. The beggar was cured instantly. He began dancing and ran into the Temple, praising God.

Those who knew him as the beggar were confounded and amazed at this. The beggar, Esau, came out and clung to Peter and John, causing more disturbance among the gathering crowd. Solomon's Portico had never witnessed such excitement before! The authorities, as usual, were looking on. Seizing this opportunity to spread the Good News and love of Jesus, Peter raised his voice above the murmuring crowds: *"Ye men of Israel, why wonder you at this? Or why look you upon us, as if by our strength or power we had made this man to walk? The God of Abraham, and the God of Isaac, and the God of Jacob, the God of our fathers, hath glorified his Son Jesus, whom you indeed delivered up and denied before the face of Pilate, when he judged he should be released. But you denied the Holy One and the Just, and desired a murderer to be granted unto you. But the author of life you killed, whom God hath raised from the dead: of which we are witnesses. And in the faith of his name, this man, whom you have seen and known, hath his name strengthened, and the faith which is by him, hath given this perfect soundness in the sight of you all."* (Acts 3:12-16)

Peter continued, "My brothers, you and your leaders acted out of ignorance. God announced through the prophets of old that the Messiah would suffer. This has been fulfilled. Therefore, reform your lives! Turn to God, that your sins may be forgiven, and *'...when the times of refreshment shall come from the presence of the Lord, and he shall send him who hath been preached unto you, Jesus Christ, Whom heaven indeed must receive, until the times of the restitution of all things, which God hath spoken by the mouth of his holy prophets, from the beginning of the world.*

For Moses said:

> *A prophet shall the Lord your God*
> *raise up unto you*
> *of your brethren, like unto me:*
> *him you shall hear according to all things*
> *whatsoever he shall speak to you.*

> *And it shall be, that every soul which will not hear*
> *that prophet, shall be destroyed from among the people.*

"'And all the prophets, from Samuel and afterwards, who have spoken, have told of these days. You are the children of the prophets and of the testament which God made to our fathers, saying to Abraham: And in thy seed shall all the kindreds of the earth be blessed. To you first, God, raising up his Son, hath sent him to bless you: that every one may convert himself from his wickedness.'" (Acts 3:20-26)

Apparently, this was all the authorities could stand since they came up to arrest them. It was evening already, so they jailed them over night. The rest of us went to our homes and began all night prayer vigils. The authorities were capable of anything and so we stayed in earnest prayer for the release of our brothers.

My son Alexander remained outside where they were held, to pray and to keep watch. Mother Mary, Mirianna (the mother of Judas Iscariot), Barnabas and a few others also stayed with him. Thousands became believers this day and so many prayers ascended to Heaven on their behalf.

The following day a multitude gathered to praise God and to pray for the release of Peter and John. I believe that the authorities were afraid of the crowd since they released the two Apostles with only a firm warning. They were forbidden to speak to anyone the name of Jesus or His teachings. It was reported that Peter responded, saying, *"If it be just, in the sight of God, to hear you rather than God, judge ye. For we cannot but speak the things which we have seen and heard."* (Acts 4:19-20)

When Peter and John came out, they told us all that had happened to them and then John raised his hands to Heaven and prayed, *"Lord, thou art he that didst make heaven and earth, the sea and all things that are in them. Who, by the Holy Ghost, by the mouth of our father David, thy servant, hast said:*

> *Why did the Gentiles rage,*
> *and the people meditate vain things?*
> *The kings of the earth stood up,*
> *and the princes assembled together*
> *against the Lord and his Christ.*

"For of a truth there assembled together in this city against thy holy child Jesus, whom thou hast anointed, Herod, and Pontius Pilate, with the Gentiles and the people of Israel, to do what thy hand and thy counsel decreed to be done. And now, Lord, behold their threatenings, and grant unto thy servants, that with all confidence they may speak thy word, by stretching forth thy hand to cures, and signs and wonders to be done by the name of thy holy Son, Jesus." (Acts 4:24-30)

When John prayed, we were in a large room across the square, and the power of the Holy Spirit overwhelmed us. The very foundation seemed to shake with an understanding of the fear and the powerful hand of God.

Solomon's Portico became our usual gathering place to instruct those who would listen. Naturally, it was the Holy Spirit Who called and drew the crowds. More cures and signs were given so that the scoffers would believe. The preaching and instructing was well proclaimed, much to the animosity of the authorities. They arrested the Apostles once again and threw them into the public jail. However, on the next day when they were to stand trial, to their amazement and anger, the jailers found them gone.

I remember looking up toward the window and seeing one of the Sadducees looking down into the courtyard, mouth opened, bewildered. Soon many were looking down. You see, during the night an Angel of the Lord released the Apostles. Once again they began to teach boldly.

Again the guards came and arrested them. Mother Mary had not slept for two days, so the women made her a little resting place where she could lie down in the shade. It took much encouragement by us for her to take the needed rest. When she finally lay down, she began moving her lips in prayer and then slept, deeply and peacefully.

Joshua, my grandson, toddled over to where Mary was and lay down next to her. Rachel kept a watchful eye on them. She remarked to me: "Father, look, even Joshua recognizes that Mary is mother of us all. He sleeps in the comfort of her serenity. Blessed is she who first held the Lord-she who bore Him and nursed Him in the cradle of her arms. Yet, how sorrowful when that comfort could not be felt at the foot of the cross. How could anyone not love and honor her."

She was so right, for Mary even declared to her cousin, Elizabeth: *". . . from henceforth all generations shall call me blessed."* (Luke 1:48) Mother Mary, above all others, could attest to the sanctity and perfection of her Divine Son. She held in her heart and mind the knowledge of those things that we shall come to know only at God's design. She was the temple in which the Lord God lived for nine months, preparing for His delivery unto the people of God.

The Sanhedrin and Sadducees thought that they had charge over the Apostles and wanted to put them to death. However, once again the voice and prayers of the people roared in their ears. If only this same roar had been heard on the day of the Crucifixion!

Esau, who had been healed, came out to tell us what had happened. Mother Mary awoke, hearing the commotion, and came over to hear what he had to say. A chair was brought for her to sit on and Alexander and Rufus, much to my joy, stood beside her. Rufus placed his hand on Mary's shoulder and she reached up with her right hand to hold his.

Esau told us: "They argued among themselves and then as the Twelve Apostles were brought before them, they said, *'We commanded you that you should not teach in this name; and behold, you have filled Jerusalem with your doctrine, and you have a mind to bring the blood of this man upon us.'* (Acts 5:28)

"The Apostles stood tall and unwavering, and after a pause, Peter spoke up and clearly boasted, *'We ought to obey God rather than men. The God of our fathers hath raised up Jesus, whom you put to death, hanging him upon a tree. Him hath God exalted with his right hand, to be Prince and Saviour. to give repentance to Israel, and remission of sins.'* (Acts 5:29-31)

"John then spoke up with conviction: *'And we are witnesses of these things and the Holy Ghost, whom God hath given to all that obey him.'* (Acts 5:32)

"Oh how they all began yelling and condemning the Twelve. The death sentence was on their lips when a Pharisee called Gamaliel ordered the Twelve out of court. Addressing the court, he stated, *'Ye men of Israel, take heed to yourselves what you intend to do, as touching these men. For before these days rose up Theodas, affirming himself to be somebody, to whom a number of men, about four hundred, joined themselves: who was slain; and all that believed him were scattered, and brought to nothing.'* (Acts 5:35-36)

"He spoke of other would-be leaders who failed and then tried to compare these with the followers of Jesus. Gamaliel continued, 'The present case is similar. My advice is that you have nothing to do with these men. Leave them alone. If their purpose and action are human in origin, they will destroy themselves. However, if they are of God, you cannot destroy them without fighting God Himself.'

"They brought the Twelve back in and commanded that they not preach the name of Jesus again. In order to show how serious they were, they had the Apostles stripped to the waist and scourged. It was so hard to witness this beating. Peter was the one who made me stand, and, through the power of God, gave me the use of my legs after some forty years.

"None of them fell to the ground in weakness but stood tall and erect in humble determination. The whip cut into their flesh several times with much force.

"John's eyes were filled with tears but his face spoke of consolation. I heard him say, 'Thank You for letting me feel the stripes heaped upon You, my Lord, which You endured for all of us. Your blessings upon us that we now receive are beyond our unworthiness. To share this is a great joy, a gift from You, Lord Jesus Christ.' They will come out soon, no doubt."

Andrew was the first to appear, accompanied by James and John. They were worn out but not withdrawn. Peter, Matthias, Matthew and the others began filing out, beaten in body but not in spirit. They were still voicing their praise of God and proclaiming the name of Jesus.

We took them home to Simeon's house and nursed their wounds. Alexander and Rufus guided John in case he became weak. In fact, all were helped through the streets with dignity. Mary and the other women hurried ahead to prepare the ointments and wrappings. As they were leaving, I noticed that Mary was carrying Joshua in her arms.

After we arrived at Simeon's house and the Apostles' wounds were dressed, Peter decided that it would be good to commemorate the Breaking of the Bread.

The women prepared the table for the Commemoration. First they washed the table and then placed a fresh linen upon it. Next, Mary placed a goblet, the one Christ Himself used for the Passover meal, and a small plate for the bread. Anna arranged the candelabra upon it and another woman brought out the wine. Mary brought some water and said, "Even the water was drained from His Body."

The men all sat around the table while the women sat in the outer circle. We began praising God and chanting Psalms. Peter then told us of how it is the command and the teaching of Jesus that we must love our enemies. Peter instructed us, saying, "Jesus said to us and to all who would listen: '. . . *to you that hear: Love your enemies, do good to them that hate you. Bless them that curse you, and pray for them that calumniate you. And to him that striketh thee on the one cheek, offer also the other. And him that taketh away from thee thy cloak, forbid not to take thy coat also. Give to every one that asketh thee, and of him that taketh away thy goods, ask them not again. And as you would that men should do to you, do you also to them in like manner. And if you love them that love you, what thanks are to you? for sinners also love those that love them. And if you do good to them who do good to you, what thanks are to you? for sinners also do this. And if you lend to them of whom you hope to receive, what thanks are to you? for sinners also lend to sinners, for to receive as much. But love ye your enemies: do good, and lend, hoping for nothing thereby: and your reward shall be great, and you shall be the sons of the Highest; for he is kind to the unthankful and to the evil. Be ye therefore merciful, as your Father also is merciful.*

"'*Judge not, and you shall not be judged. Condemn not, and you shall not be condemned. Forgive, and you shall be forgiven. Give, and it shall be given to you: good measure and pressed down and shaken together and running over shall they give into your bosom. For with the same measure that you shall mete withal, it shall be measured to you again.*'" (Luke 6:27-38)

Peter continued, "We have seen today that our persecution is only beginning. Hatred for our enemies is what would be expected of us. But we have climbed above the normal and into the spiritual with Jesus, Our Lord. There can be no place in our hearts for anything but love; yes, even for our enemies. They have refused to take the blinders from their eyes and would rather live in darkness than walk freely in the light.

"We have seen the light and so we live in the light. Once we have seen the light how could we ever seek to live in darkness again. We must continue to preach and to teach all who will listen. They can destroy our bodies, which belong to the earth, but not our souls, which will live eternally in the Resurrection."

"My brothers and sisters," Peter exclaimed, "let us offer up the Remembrance of Christ's sacrifice and death and commemorate the words He spoke at our last meal with Him. Let us offer up the bread and the wine as Jesus did."

The Apostles and those chosen by them as priests were assembled at the head of the table. They were set apart, and yet remained very much a part of us. They were very special, dedicated to the Lord as were the Apostles. The Apostles were chosen by Christ. By the laying on of their hands, others became the chosen of Christ as well. These men, called *priests*, would be the extension of the Apostles who stand in the place of Christ. Only they have the authority to proclaim and carry out this awesome Mystery of the bread and wine becoming the very Body and Blood, Soul and Divinity of Jesus. In Genesis it is said, ***"But Melchisedech the king of Salem, bringing forth bread and wine, for he was the priest of the most high God, Blessed him, and said: Blessed be Abram..."*** (Genesis 14:18) And again in Psalm 109 it is declared: ***"Thou art a priest for ever according to the order of Melchisedech."*** (Pslam 109:4)

These words I heard over and over again, each time a new priest was prayed over. It would be the joy of a father to know that his son gave such humble submission to the Father through and in the Son of God, Jesus Most Holy.

Oh, Rufus, if only the Lord would bless you to stand counted among this special priesthood, the Priesthood of Melchizedek.

All the Apostles and priests raised their hands toward the bread, and in turn toward the wine, as Peter lifted them up toward the very heavens. These gifts were raised to meet the Holy Spirit, Whom Christ has sent in order that this bread no longer remains bread and this wine no longer remains wine, but becomes rather the very Body and Blood of Him Who was crucified for us. It is by this Blood that we are protected forever.

Peter repeated the words we hear at every Breaking of the Bread: *"And whilst they were at supper, Jesus took bread, and blessed and broke: and gave to his disciples, and said: Take ye, and eat. This is my body."* (Matt. 26:26)

Taking up the very goblet that Christ had used he said, *"Drink ye all of this. For this is my blood of the new testament, which shall be shed for many unto remission of sins. And I say to you, I will not drink from henceforth of this fruit of the vine until that day when I shall drink it with you new in the kingdom of my Father."* (Matt. 26:27-29)

Each time I'm present, my eyes remain on the very Body and Blood of our Risen Savior. Each time we come to the altar of Christ's Sacrifice, my heart is lifted up and my eyes fill with tears of supreme joy. I recalled when first, in my unworthiness, Mary led me to the altar. As I saw this most awesome gift come toward me, the *hands of Christ Himself* gave it to me, for those hands had the marks of the nails. My soul cried out in ecstasy and praise. I heard the sweet sound of the angelic chorus all around me. I saw my precious Lord. I partook and I shared in His most precious Body and Blood.

Lord Jesus Christ, You were made obedient unto death, and Your name is exalted above all others. Teach me always to do the Father's will so that made holy by obedience, which unites all of us to the Sacrifice of Your Body, we can expect Your great love in times of sorrow and sing a new song to our God. Amen

The Disciples of the Lord grew and grew, as pleased the Lord, and also the realization that there was a great need for assistance. The Disciples numbered among the Greeks complained that their widows were being neglected in the daily distribution of food, while the Hebrew widows seemed to receive assistance first.

The Apostles gathered the community together and told them to settle this dispute in charity. Andrew voiced his concern over the squabble, saying, *"It is not reason that we should leave the word of God and serve tables. Wherefore, brethren, look ye out among you seven men of good reputation, full of the Holy Ghost and wisdom, whom we may appoint over this business. But we will give ourselves continually to prayer and to the ministry of the word."* (Acts 6:2-4)

The community accepted this proposal and set about discerning who to choose. Finally, the selection began, and the first deacon to be chosen was Stephen, a very holy man of God. He was filled with the Holy Spirit. He was selected from the beginning to take charge and direct the others: Philip, Prochrus, Nicanor, Timon, Parmenas, and Nicolaus of Antioch, who had been a convert to Judaism. After being presented to the Apostles and accepted by them as worthy, they laid hands on them and ordained them deacons of the Lord.

These new deacons began their work with deep commitment to the Lord. Stephen set up special programs for the widows of Hebrews and Greeks. With help from the others, he also set up charitable ways to help the poor who could not live in a communal setting. Both Disciples of the Lord and those who were of other beliefs were aided. Because of this true act of love and charity, many more people came to accept Jesus Christ. Among those baptized were counted many priests from among the Jews.

Stephen was eventually arrested, taken out of the city and stoned to death. Although his ministry was cut short, much had been accomplished. When Stephen stood before the high priest, he instructed and scolded him. No doubt his words were from the Holy Spirit.

When he was nearly finished, his soul was totally aflame with the glory of God. His mission was to do just this: witness faithfully unto the Lord. He looked up to Heaven, and seeing the Glory of God, he began to speak with great strength and conviction: *"Behold, I see the heavens opened, and the Son of man standing on the right hand of God."* (Acts 7:55)

This was more than the hypocrites could accept and they cursed him and covered their ears so that they could hear no more.

Like a pack of wild beasts they jumped him and dragged him outside the city walls where they stoned him to death.

He was thrown to the ground, but then he rose to a kneeling
position and raised his arms in submission to the Lord. The high
priest then threw the first stone, hitting him in the lower back. At
that, Stephen stood up with much difficulty. There was a pause as
the murderers wondered what would happen next. They knew in
their inner most selves that this was an honest and holy man. As
he stood, he asked God: "In the name of Jesus, forgive these spir-
itually- crippled tormentors."

At that they feared him even more and a stream of rocks came
at him from all directions. His body, broken from the blows, fell
to the ground as he uttered, *"Lord Jesus, receive my spirit."* (Acts
7:58)

His face reflected ecstasy rather than suffering, for he kept his
eyes on the Lord. Close to death now, he proclaimed in a loud
voice: *"Lord, lay not this sin to their charge."* (Acts 7:59)

Those were his last words and they expressed the true forgiveness that Christ taught. For even as the Lord hung dying on
the cross, He asked the Father: *"Father, forgive them, for they
know not what they do."* (Luke 23:34)

Other deacons were soon ordained by the Apostles and I'm
proud to say that both Alexander and Rufus were among them.
The persecution became wide spread throughout the area and
many Disciples fled to various areas away from Jerusalem.
Alexander and Rufus went first to Cyrene and then to Cyprus and
Antioch.

Before his death, Stephen paved the way for missionaries to
go to Phoenicia, Cyprus and Antioch, but they preached only to
the Jews. Alexander and Rufus began preaching to the Greeks
about the good news of Jesus. With the power of the Holy Spirit,
many came to believe.

In Jerusalem they heard of the wonderful happenings in
Antioch and the Apostle Barnabas was sent to see how things
truly were. Barnabas was overjoyed at what he witnessed and he
began preaching and instructing as well. The increase in converts
was outstanding.

He was unable to stay long with them because he was look-ing for Paul, who had led the persecutions until the Lord Himself converted him. While Barnabas was preparing for his journey, he decided that it was necessary to leave a priest with the Antiochian community. Of the deacons who had worked there, Alexander and Rufus were both selected for Ordination.

I had long prayed that Rufus would one day be a priest of Christ, but to realize that Alexander had also been called was beyond my most fervent prayers. If only I could have been there to witness this special gift. In Jerusalem we rejoiced over the news.

Their wives and children eventually joined them. I missed them but we must all be about the Lord's work. I had hoped that they might find some protection from the persecution that was so prominent.

Eventually Barnabas and Paul arrived in Antioch from Tarsus, where Paul was found. They were very proud of the work Alexander and Rufus had accomplished.

Barnabas and Paul stayed on in Antioch for over a year. It was here that the Disciples of Christ were first called Christians.

CHAPTER 6

You Are A Priest Forever

Jacob, my cousin, I fear that they will come before long and I shall go to meet my Lord and Master. So, I must write down the events of these last days. (From Simon's final letter to his cousin Jacob)

Two years ago John asked me to go to Cyrene to help with the Christian community there. Many of the deacons and priests had been arrested and martyred for the Faith. In some areas whole communities were martyred. The price of our Faith became our blood.

Many died with deep faith and hope in what was awaiting them. For them it was not the beastly act of death but a joyful crossing over to be with Christ. How could a man who preached only peace and love become so hated! They tried to wipe out His memory but instead saw it increase over the whole world.

Put us to death and hear us sing on the way! Do not cry for us for we go to the promise of our eternal home. Death is only a brief transition from this world to the next.

"Simon," John began, "I want to send you to Cyrene as a missionary of the Gospel of Christ. They need a shepherd to guide them and to offer the Sacrifice of Calvary upon the altar; to instruct them and to give consolation to the penitent and the dying; to bless the union of Christian men and women and to baptize those who come to the Faith of Christ. "You will lay hands on them and call down upon them the Holy Spirit's anointing. You will be the voice of Christ, bringing the good news of salvation to all who will hear. Through the power of the Holy Spirit, you will bring the very Body and Blood, Soul and Divinity to the deserv-

ing souls in your care. Simon, do you feel equal to this calling by
Our Lord?"

Without hesitation I said, "Yes." After all these years, the
Lord was calling *me* to the highest honor! I would be ordained
and begin the journey in about six weeks.

There was someone I wanted to visit before I left. Mother
Mary was now living in Nazareth with Mary, the sister of
Lazarus, whom Christ once raised from the dead. There was quite
a large community of Christians there, as well as many relatives
of Mother Mary.

She lived in the very house in which Jesus lived throughout
His life. This house was blessed with the lives of Mary, Joseph
and Jesus. The blessed memories that are held within those walls!

Once Jesus visited Nazareth and was expelled because of the
hardness of the hearts of even His own relations. A prophet is
never recognized in his own village. But now many had turned to
Him and believed.

In the distance, the silhouette of Nazareth began to take
shape. My heart beat quickly and hard at the knowledge that I
really would be at Mary's home, the home of my Savior and Lord,
walking those same streets where Jesus once ran and played with
His friends.

It was in Nazareth that Jesus learned the art of carpentry
from his foster father, Joseph. Such a guardian Joseph must have
been, to be elected by almighty God to protect Mary and Jesus
throughout his lifetime. He was a hard worker, to be sure. We
know so little about him, and yet, his role, although silent, was
so very important. He, too, had to offer his *fiat* to God. He heard
God's call and answered without question. Aside from the
Almighty Father, the Lord our God, was any man a better father
or protector?

Such a holy family: the perfect parents chosen by God to care
for the perfect Son, His Son, God Come Down, Emmanuel, God
With Us! The Almighty One must have chosen them long before
Abraham was conceived in the womb of his mother. For God is
orderly and sets His plans outside of time as we know it. The
woman whom God chose to be the mother of His Son was, no
doubt, a special creation herself. She was to be the tabernacle in

which the Lord God, by means of His Holy Spirit, would place the Son, God Incarnate. For nine months this tabernacle fed and nourished the Messiah with her very own body and blood, protecting Him, loving God within and without!

Jesus, at the Last Supper, gave us His precious Body and Blood so that we might have life and have it to the fullest. Without this precious Food, we would surely die. This Mother Mary did for Him by the means of her own body. It is nothing strange, for all mothers with child do the same. The difference is that this mother fed God Himself in the embryo of His Son. Praise be to God Almighty for His great love for His creation!

Some small children came running to me as I reached the gate of Nazareth. A little girl, accompanied by three small boys, was the first to speak to me: "Have you come from far away?" she asked with eyes round with wonder.

One of the boys asked, "Are you from Jerusalem?"

Another boy, who was very round and jolly, smiled and said, "Hi, my name is Mark, and this is my sister Ruth, and my cousins, Benjamin and Ramier. We saw you coming from far away and wanted to greet you!"

"Well then," I replied, "shalom!'

The children returned my greeting and asked who I came to see. "I have come to visit Mary, the mother of Jesus Bar Joseph the Carpenter."

Even these little ones knew who I meant. Ruth exclaimed, "You mean Mother Mary?"

Little Benjamin chimed in: "She is our best friend! When our mother was killed and our father went to work in the salt mines, Mother Mary took us into her own home. Come with us and we will take you home."

Mark asked if Mother Mary knew I was coming and then ran ahead without waiting for an answer. They had many questions, but being typical children, they scarcely waited for the answers in their great excitement.

As we approached the house, Mark was sitting on the step and Mary was standing in the doorway. When she recognized me, she became very excited and ran to meet me, embracing me in motherly affection.

"My son," for so she called us all, "how happy I am to see you! It has been so long. Now you are here. How long can you stay?"

I told her that I could stay only one night and then must return to Jerusalem. She was so excited about the adventures I had encountered since we last saw one another. But the news of why I was there was very precious to her and tears came to her eyes.

"Simon, you have come so far in your journey with my precious Son, our Lord and Savior. Now you are to become a shepherd of the flock of God's special children. Every day you will be able to present Jesus to the believers through the action of the Holy Spirit."

She reached out, and grabbing my hands, led me to sit at her table. Then she continued to speak softly, sincerely, with the voice of authority: "These hands will hold my Son every day when you offer the Sacrifice of His Body and Blood as He requested during His Last Supper. These hands will become *His* hands in healing and consoling; in guiding and in giving to all who are in need. Your faith and example will shine forth and bring others to the realization that you already know."

She released my hands and looked into my eyes, which had filled with tears. She continued, "There is one sure way, Simon, to keep firm in the goodness of Jesus for always, and that is to love God with all your soul, all your heart and all your mind, and to work for Him alone. Then God will give you strength and joy. The yoke of God will be sweet and light for you, and in adversity, by struggling and persevering, you will gradually become stronger and stronger, living fully in Christ and fearing no evil of any sort."

Mary arose from her chair and fetched some bread and wine. "Here, my son, eat and drink to nourish the body. Jesus will continue to nourish your soul with Heavenly Food."

She went into another room and returned with a white linen folded several times. She sat down across from me and handed me the linen. "Take this," she said, "and use it every time you commemorate His Body and Blood. This is the very linen He ate

His last meal upon. I have had it these years but now it goes into your safe keeping."

I thanked her, recalling that day when she presented me with one of His nails. Reaching for the little pouch I wore around my neck, I pulled out that nail. "Ah! You still have this instrument of His love. Never part with this treasure except to pass it on when the time has come."

As we sat and talked about times past, Benjamin and Ramier came inside. They ran to us and standing on either side of Mary, they asked if I was going to stay with them. "Well, of course! He will share your room. And by the way, isn't it past your bedtime?"

The sun was on the horizon, preparing to say its own good-night. Time had slipped away during our conversation and the day was gone. The children wanted me to tell them of far-off places, an adventure of some kind. I noticed that Mary looked tired and so I bid her goodnight and retired with the children. After telling them their story and tucking them into their beds, I stretched out my bed roll and prepared to sleep. The day's events and the special grace I had received were still flowing through my mind and heart. I must have lain there for over two hours because the moon was now high in the sky. From the other room, I could hear Mary's voice as she prayed the Psalms and spoke to her Son. She was still praying when sleep finally stole my senses.

As the new day began to break, I heard Mary in prayer once again. Had she kept vigil throughout the night? Finally, she came to the draped doorway of the children's room and sang a soft praise to the Father. The children awoke and sang back a response. The next thing I knew, they were out of their beds and on top of me, calling, "Come on, sleepy head, it's time to rise with the sun and praise the Son of God!" How beautiful are these little ones. How fortunate are they to have such an adoptive mother-no, rather a true mother of such love.

Mary had breakfast ready and was setting the table. After giving thanks to the Creator, we ate a humble breakfast. The children and I cleaned up when we were done while Mary disappeared into her room.

Then a woman named Helena came to the door and said, "Greetings unto this house of the Lord where His mercy endures."

I introduced myself but she already knew who I was. "Mary came over early this morning and asked if I would care for the children while she is away, so here I am," she said.

Just then Mary came out of her room, carrying a small satchel and exclaimed to me: "Simon, we must start now so that we arrive in Jerusalem at a reasonable hour." I had no idea that she planned to accompany me to Jerusalem, but, of course, I was delighted that the mother of my Lord should desire to be present at my Ordination.

I reminded her, however, that the trip would be long and tiring for her. "Simon, Simon! I would travel any distance to be with my children; especially, when they are preparing to give themselves totally to God the Father through Jesus Christ, our Lord. My heart yearns for all of you, and a special place is reserved there for all your joys, sorrows, hurts, triumphs and needs. A mother's heart has room for each and every child.

"Simon, I hold you close to my heart and want to share your joy. My Son will stand with you every day of your life. The gifts that you will receive and give to others will be very special. I want to be present for this joyous occasion in your life. Your own mother was never able to share with you your *rebirth*, so please, let me do this for you. Let me be your mother-in-attendance to share this joy." So much love filled these words.

I felt so small at that moment. Not because of my desire to save her the long journey, but because I truly felt like her little child-a child who is loved so much by his mother.

Mary turned toward the children and Helena, saying, "Benjamin and Ramier, I will be gone for a while so Helena will be watching over you. Your Aunt Mary," (she who is the sister of Lazarus), "will be home in a few days and relieve Helena. I know you will be on your best behavior and take care of our home. I love you both very much and will miss you." The children and Mary then embraced with tender affection.

The little ones held back their tears, and Ramier said, "Mother, we will ask Jesus to watch over you and Simon and keep you both safe. We love you, too, this much." He opened his arms as wide as he could. Although he smiled brightly, a tear swelled in the corner of his eye.

After bidding farewell to the children and Helena, we were off. Mary rode on a donkey as I walked along side her. I felt proud, yet, humble, to travel with Mother Mary. These moments I treasure in my heart.

After reaching Jerusalem, we went directly to the house of Simeon. John was expecting me but was overjoyed to see my traveling companion. Food had been prepared, awaiting the hour of my arrival. We ate and then retired for the night.

In the morning, Mary rose early and went to the Temple to offer thanks for our safe journey. As she was entering, she saw a small child cowering in the corner. "What's wrong, my little one?" she asked. Mary went over to her and sitting down on the floor, took the child into her arms.

"My mommy and daddy were killed by some mean men. They came to our house and called them all kinds of names because we love Jesus Christ. They grabbed Mommy and started hitting her in the face and stomach. Other men held Daddy and they made him watch what they did to Mommy.

"I was hiding under a basket so they couldn't see me. Then they took Mommy," she sobbed, "and kept kicking her until blood was all over. Mommy had my little brother in her stomach and the men said, 'That baby will never be a Christian!'

"Another man cut my mother's neck with a knife. Then they killed Daddy."

Mary wept with the child over this horrible madness, this insane hatred. She picked the child up and brought her to Simeon's. This little one was adopted by Mary and returned with her to Nazareth.

How could we ever understand the fullness of evil that corrupts some men's hearts? Our hearts are ruled by the redeeming force of God's love. We must work so diligently to spread the teachings of the Master. He is the source of everything, even our very lives. Of course they can take our bodies, but never our souls. Our souls live in the fullness of Christ.

John, Matthew and James suggested to Mary that she should leave Jerusalem as soon as possible for her own safety and that of the child. She insisted, however, that they would be safe and would leave after my Ordination. She could be very determined and was never afraid of what anyone could do to her physically. She would often say, "This life is but a transition to the next where we will live eternally with God the Father and Jesus. If men help us reach that ultimate joy sooner than expected, then God's Will be done."

And they agreed, "So be it."

That evening Simeon asked me to go with him to a storage room downstairs. He said, "Simon, there are many things that you will need to take with you on your trip. Here you will find everything needed, as well as supplies that might be useful for the community at Cyrene. I'll arrange for a special caravan for you to travel with."

I stayed for sometime going through the supplies and preparing them for travel. Simeon had told me that I would be leaving sooner than anticipated.

The next day news came to us that several of the Jerusalem community had been arrested on charges of treason. Persecution was rampant and Christians were being horribly dealt with. Several deacons were put to death. Any leaders, especially the ministers, were targeted for cruel and inhuman deaths.

A small gathering took place in the Upper Room and after prayers and the Commemoration of the Lord's Supper, we discussed the teachings of Jesus.

Then Clement, a priest of Christ, arrived with further news. The news he had was from Antioch. There had been a raid on several gatherings in that area, and many people were killed, including the deacons and priests who cared for them. As he told us of the massacre and martyrdom of our fellow disciples, my heart burst in sorrow. Alexander and Rufus were among the martyred. Mother Mary held me, for I had fallen to my knees. I trembled and the tears began to flow uncontrollably from my eyes. My heart was torn to shreds.

John asked about Rachel and Naomi, and we learned that they, too, along with Naomi's child, my granddaughter, my darling Jolema's little namesake, had also died in the name of Jesus.

Suddenly, a small voice was heard crying out, "Grandfather! Grandfather!" It was Joshua.

Clement had brought Joshua with him. The child had been spared because he was outside the village, playing with friends. He hid when he realized what had happened. Perplexed about what to do with Joshua, I turned to John for help. He encouraged me to let Joshua go with Mary to Nazareth.

It was the safest and best decision. But after all this time, and now, in the present situation, how could I part with my only surviving grandchild. My heart was pierced with great sorrow. My children were dead. My thoughts were not equal to the situation at hand. Tomorrow I would need to make a decision. Until then we would spend good time together this night.

The following morning, Simeon came to wake me. "Simon. Simon, arise and prepare the donkeys for the journey. Mother Mary is up and has the children ready. John, Mirianna and I will escort them to Nazareth. When all is ready, come back to the Upper Room and prepare for your Ordination."

Plans had changed once again because of the rising tide of events. But there was joy at the thought of my impending Ordination.

I had decided that Joshua would stay with Mother Mary. She could be more family to him than I, and he would be brought up to serve the Lord in all ways. The road that I would travel was not for a child. I'm sure his parents would be pleased with this decision.

Mary would take both children to Nazareth and raise them. Eventually she started several houses where children could live with loving adoptive parents. Many Gentile Christians adopted Jewish Christian children. This became such a valuable ministry because so many children lost their relatives. Of course, many children also met martyrdom.

Now all was ready and the assembly was gathered in the Upper Room. James presided since he was head of the Church in Jerusalem. He sat in a chair near the altar with John and Thomas on either side. Dressed in my best tunic, I walked humbly towards James, escorted by Mark. The rays of the sun were splashing through the window upon the altar behind the Apostles.

Everything the sun touched was arrayed in golden hues. I felt warm all over, not from heat, but from the Mighty Presence of Jesus and the Holy Spirit.

I approached James, knelt and bowed my head to the floor in total submission to Christ my Savior. Suddenly, I heard the most beautiful voice raised in celestial splendor, singing Psalm Sixty-Seven. The voice was that of Mother Mary:

> *May God have mercy on us, and bless us:*
>   *may he cause the light of his countenance*
>   *to shine upon us, and may he have mercy on us.*
> *That we may know thy way upon earth:*
>   *thy salvation in all nations.*
> *Let people confess to thee, O God:*
>   *let all people give praise to thee.* (Psalm 66:1-4)

James began, "We rely on the help of the Lord God and our Savior Jesus Christ, and we choose this man, Simon, our brother, to the office of presbyter, to go out among the community of Cyrene and where ever the Lord shall draw him. Our brother is to serve Christ the Teacher, Priest and Shepherd, in ministry that is to make Christ's own Body, the Church, grow through the people of God. He is called to share in our own priesthood and to be molded into the likeness of Christ. By consecration he will be made a true priest of the Scriptures and teacher of the teachings of Christ. He will sustain God's people and commemorate the Lord's Sacrifice.

"Simon, my son, you must apply your energies to the duty of teaching the holy name of Jesus, the chief Teacher. Share with all mankind the Word of God you have received with joy. Let the doctrine you teach be true nourishment for the people of God. Let the example of your life attract the followers of Christ, so that by word and action you may build up the house which is God's Church.

"Your ministry will perfect the spiritual and physical sacrifice of the faithful by uniting it to Christ's Sacrifice, the Sacrifice of Calvary, which is now to be offered through your hands. Finally, conscious of sharing in the work of Christ, seek to bring the faithful together in a unified family and to lead them effectively, through Christ and the Holy Spirit, to God the Father. Always remember the example of the Good Shepherd, who came not to be served but to serve and to rescue those who were lost."

My spirit rejoiced in the Lord my God as the sun's rays flowed through the open window, its golden hue embracing all of us. A fresh breeze filtered through the room, gently touching my face. James stood up and raised his hands toward Heaven and prayed, "Hear us, O Lord our God, and pour out upon Your servant, Simon, the blessing of the Holy Spirit and the grace and power of the priesthood of Your Son, Jesus Christ. Support him with Your unending love."

The power of the Holy Spirit overwhelmed me and my whole body began to tremble in its powerful recognition. James then placed his hands upon my head and continued to pray: "Come to our help, Lord, holy Father, almighty and eternal God, for You are the Source of every goodness. When You appointed high priests to rule Your people, You chose other men next to them in rank and dignity to be with them and to help them in their task, and so there grew up the ranks of priests and the office of Levites, established by sacred rites.

"In the desert you extended the spirit of Moses to seventy wise men who helped him rule the great company of his people. You shared among the sons of Aaron the fullness of their father's power to provide worthy priests in sufficient number for the increasing rites of sacrifice and worship. With the same loving care, you gave companions to Your Son's Apostles to help in teaching the Faith. Lord, grant also to us such fellow workers, for we are weak and our need is becoming very great. May he be faithful in working with us so that the words of the Gospel may reach the whole of the earth."

Mother Mary rose from her seat and brought forth a stole and outer garment of a precious material. I did not know at the time that she had been awake all night, preparing them for today. They were made by her own hands. Mark placed them on me as a symbol of priestly authority.

After instructing me to place my hands in those of James, a special oil was used to anoint them. James prayed, "The Father anointed our Lord Jesus Christ through the power of the Holy Spirit. May Jesus preserve you to sanctify the Christian people and to offer sacrifice to God. *Simon, you are a priest forever, according to the line of Melchizedek."*

As I arose, everyone came forward to receive a special blessing. Mother Mary was one of the first. She kissed my hands and I remembered all the things she had told me in Nazareth.

Mary and the other women had prepared a simple meal before the ceremony, for two reasons: in celebration and in preparation for our journeys. Joshua understood why he could not come with me and he spent the remainder of this time enjoying the company of the other children.

As for me, I had much work to do: deserts to cross and souls to save for Jesus Christ. A new surge of commitment rallied in my soul. Determined to serve my Lord, no matter what befell me, I set my course for Cyrene.

There were about one hundred travelers in the caravan. Many were Christians, returning home, and now I was to be their priest. Claudius, a deacon from Jerusalem, was to be one of my assistants. The leader of the caravan was not Christian but several in his family were. He was a stubborn sort, but he loved his family, Christian or not. Eventually, he, too, would be baptized.

I spent nearly two years in Cyrene, ministering to the community of believers. Many came to know the Messiah and were baptized. We never knew when the authorities would come but we did not let that stop us.

Our aid to widows continued without hindrance, as did our many other charitable ministries. Several families took in the children who had lost their parents in the horrendous persecutions. Some felt that we should not care for those who were not Christian, but soon they began to realize that according to the teachings of Jesus, we must love all.

CHAPTER 7

Cyrene: The Last Days

It was a joy and a privilege to be their priest. However, the most joyful act, the most sublime act, was that of offering the Sacrifice of Christ's love. It wasn't until our arrival in Cyrene that I first offered this Action of Divine Mercy. If time yet permits, Jacob, I wish to introduce you to this great Sacrifice through my own recollections. (From Simon's final letter to his cousin Jacob)

I had been in Cyrene for three days, meeting my brothers and sisters in Christ and learning of their needs, both spiritual and physical. I instructed all to come to the home of Marcellus, where Claudius and myself would live also.

Word spread among the believers that those who were well-to-do should bring items of charity for the poor. Clothing, fabrics, food, tools and money were to be collected and shared in a communal way. This would happen on the first day of the week called *Sun-day,* the day of the week on which Christ's Resurrection took place.

On that day the community arrived, bearing all sorts of things that would be distributed among the poor. Rich and poor alike arrived and brought what they were able. The poor brought whatever they counted as excess, although I believe that often this was a great burden to them. All these gifts were placed around the altar, for they were to be offered first to the Father for His blessing upon them.

On that day I prayed, "In all that we offer, we bless the Creator of the universe through His Son Jesus Christ and through the Holy Spirit."

On that day several children and adults were baptized in the Lord. Claudius, Marcellus and I poured water on the heads of the new believers, saying, "In the name of Jesus Christ, in Whom we live and die, I pour this water upon you to cleanse you of all your transgressions and to give you new birth, in the name of the Father, the Son, and the Holy Spirit."

When all had been baptized, prayers of thanks were given. We prayed fervently together for ourselves, for those who had just been enlightened, and for all the rest, where ever they might be, that having come to know the truth, all might be judged worthy to practice good works, keep the Commandments and so obtain everlasting salvation.

When these prayers were finished, we gave one another the kiss of Christ's peace. Then the teachings of Christ and the Apostles, those friends who lived and traveled with Him, were proclaimed, along with the writings of the Prophets and the Psalms.

Then I exhorted the community: "Listen well, my brothers and sisters. How different is the heart of Christ, which is open to every human being, to heal every suffering, to see so much value in every heart that He never refused forgiveness to anyone, never refused His help to anyone. He did not hesitate to die for us sinners, however ungrateful we might be. Suffering was intended by God to be one of the noblest things on earth. Therefore, Jesus chose it willingly. It should purify and refine us and make us beautiful of soul. Each pain and trouble can bring us closer to Christ; each sorrow or hurt feeling or personal problem can become an act of faith and love. It can open us and make us free. The gift Jesus made of Himself on the cross was the greatest act of freedom. He chose it willingly out of pure, generous love.

"With ever increasing intensity, the Sacrifice we now offer prepares us for the great Paschal Mystery. This day Isaiah reminds us of the meekness and humility of how Jesus went to His passion and death:

> *I have given my body to the strikers,*
>
> *and my cheeks to them that plucked them:*
>
> *I have not turned away my face from them that rebuked me, and spit upon me.* (Isaiah 50:6)

"At the same time, Isaiah indicates how these sufferings are His glory:

> **The Lord GOD is my helper,**
> **therefore I am not confounded.** (Isaiah 50:7)

"The passion of Christ was very painful as I have witnessed, but it was not a disgrace. Christ looked forward to it. Jesus said, 'My time is near. I am to celebrate the Passover with My Disciples.'

"He was indeed to celebrate the new and perfect Passover, the total gift of Himself, so that with Him we, too, might pass over from death to life. We share that Passover best when we do it in the Spirit of Jesus. He gave Himself that we might live. He emptied Himself, to glorify us. Are we willing to drink of the cup He drank?

"Do we sincerely try to empty ourselves, to throw out some of that self love, so that He can enter in? Is the refuse of narrow prejudice removed, so that we are open to share anything with Him Who opened Himself to die for us all? Unless we truly share in His Spirit of generosity and total self giving, we cannot really take part in what Christ is doing in this Mystery of our Faith. Nor can we really feel the very special joy which sharing in the cross can bring us."

I'm not sure just how long I spoke, for the Holy Spirit of God was upon me. It was He Who gave me utterance. Although I lack formal education, the Lord has provided an education that He alone nurtures within me.

After the address to the community, I approached the altar and we prayed that God would accept all that we do in the name of Jesus, His Son. Bread as is used at Passover was brought to the altar with wine and water. These were to be placed upon the altar and used for His Commemoration. The altar was covered with the very linen that was used at the Last Supper, the one given to me by Mary. What bliss, what sorrow, what joy-this gift used by Jesus Himself! The nail was also upon the altar-the same nail that had fastened Him to the cross.

I prayed, "Let us attend and stand well; let us stand in awe; let us be attentive to offer the Holy Oblation in peace."

The community responded, "A mercy of peace; a sacrifice of praise."

"The grace of Our Lord Jesus Christ, the love of God the Father, and the Communion of the Holy Spirit be with you all."

"And with your spirit."

"Let us lift up our hearts."

"We lift them up to the Lord."

"Let us give thanks to the Lord."

"It is fitting and right to worship the Father, the Son and the Holy Spirit, One in substance and undivided."

Then holding the bread I offered thanks, saying,: "We give Thee thanks, our Father, for the life and the knowledge that Thou has revealed to us through Jesus, Thy Child. Glory to Thee forever!"

Holding the cup of wine and water I prayed, "We give Thee thanks, our Father, for the holy Vine of David Thy servant that Thou has revealed to us through Jesus, Thy Child. Glory to Thee forever!"

I felt a surge of great peace and love fill my heart and soul and filter through my whole being. I continued the prayers: "Just as this bread which we break, once scattered over the hills, has been gathered and made one, so may Thy Church, too, be assembled from the ends of the earth into Thy Kingdom. For glory and power are Thine forever! No one is to eat or drink Your Eucharist except those who have been baptized in the name of the Lord; for in this regard the Lord said: 'Do not give holy things to the dogs.'

"Holy, holy, holy, Lord of the universe, Heaven and earth are filled with Your glory. Hosanna in the highest."

Then I prayed silently: "O Lord Jesus Christ, who am I that I should stand here and offer this sublime and perfect Sacrifice? Please, come and use me as Thy instrument, and let Thy Holy Spirit empower me to do Thy perfect will."

My heart beat loudly and hurriedly, while my body felt, light as a feather, as if it were floating upon a cloud.

"When He gave Himself up willingly to suffering to destroy death, to break the fetters of the devil, to trample hell under His feet, to spread His light abroad over the just, to establish the

Covenant and manifest His Resurrection, He took bread." I picked up the bread and raised it toward Heaven and then brought it back and spoke His words over it: *"This is my body, which is given for you. Do this for a commemoration of me."* (Luke 22:19)

I then lifted the chalice and prayed, *"This is the chalice, the new testament in my blood, which shall be shed for you."* (Luke 22:20)

My hands trembled as I held His precious Body and Blood. As I spoke those words, I saw angels in attendance, bowing low with their heads touching the ground. My ears were filled with the celestial harmony of the choirs of these same angels. In my hands the Bread became like a miniature sun, radiating streams of glory, covering all those who were attending. Upon raising the cup, these effects continued, the streams of glory going forth. Could it be that these glorious streams were the very streams of Christ's Blood shed on the cross-the Blood that saves us and covers us to purify our very souls; His Divine Love; His Divine Mercy; His Salvation poured out upon us? Have I witnessed the perfection of God's undying love, that He would send us His only Son to suffer and die for us all?

"We then, remembering Thy death and Thy Resurrection, offer Thee Bread and Wine. We give Thee thanks for having judged us worthy to stand before Thee and serve Thee. And we beg Thee to send Thy Holy Spirit upon the offering of Thy holy Church, to gather and unite all who receive It. May they be filled with the Holy Spirit Who strengthens their faith in the Truth. So may we be able to praise and glorify Thee through Thy Child, Jesus Christ. Through Him, glory to Thee, and honor to the Father and to the Son, with the Holy Spirit, in Thy holy Church now and forever. Amen.

"Come unto the throne and grace of God to receive this precious gift of His love. Even this, the very Body and Blood of Jesus Christ, our Lord."

When this most sanctified Bread and Wine, this very Body and Blood had been given to the people by the deacons and myself, we offered great thanksgiving and rejoicing. Our wholeness at this moment was complete and we praised God with every fiber of our body and soul. If only you could come to accept these awesome mysteries left to us for all times.

We call this food *Eucharist.* No one can have a share in It unless he has undergone the Washing which forgives sins and regenerates, and unless he lives according to the teaching of Christ. For we do not take this Food as though it were ordinary bread and wine, but, just as through the Word of God, Jesus Christ became Incarnate, taking flesh and blood for our salvation, in the same way, this Food, which has become Eucharist, thanks to the prayer formed out of the words of Christ, and which nourishes and is assimilated into our flesh and blood, is the Flesh and Blood of Incarnate Jesus. *This* is the *Truth* that we have received.

For, indeed, the Apostles' very words tell us that Jesus gave them this command: "Having taken bread, He gave thanks and said, 'Do this in memory of Me. This is My Body;' in the same way, having taken the cup, He gave thanks and said, 'This is My Blood.'" It was to them, His Apostles, that He first gave this command, and it is through them, His Apostles, that we lowly priests have been given this authority to commemorate this action.

As long as there exists and unbroken line of this Apostolic Succession from Apostle to bishop, bishops will continue to ordain priests to carry on this work.

Here in Cyrene we were graced with a lengthy period of peace with our non-Christian neighbors. Of course, it was our practice to treat all with love and compassion. This moved many to explore the teachings of Jesus. Yet, as always, there were those who would not accept any common ground.

One day Claudius and Marcellus were visiting the sick to bring the Eucharist to them. In the outlying areas they came upon a house where an elderly couple lived. Because of their age they needed someone to care for their physical needs. A lady named Amata was taking care of them and took control of the household. She was a recent convert to the Faith, although she seemed to follow her own way.

As Marcellus and Claudius entered the open door, they found the house had been ransacked. They looked for the elderly couple, finding them both lying in the sand behind the house. The woman had been killed and the man was near death. They had been robbed by their housekeeper, obviously a Christian in name only. With his last breath, the old man told us what he could.

"Amata became the daughter we never had," he said. "She said that we Christians were going to pay for. . . ." He stopped speaking, took a slow, long breath, and uttered these last words: "O my Jesus, have mercy and receive your servant." As he spoke, his eyes opened wide, he smiled gently, and died.

Little did we know that Amata had actually come to see what was happening in the Christian community. I'm sure that her lies about us to the authorities created this present surge of persecution in our village. I pray that God will visit His mercy upon her.

Marcellus and Claudius began preparing the community for another persecution. We spent much time in prayer and each day offered the Sacrifice of Calvary. From this we received our strength and acceptance of whatever fate would come.

Other than this, we went about our normal activities. In the Lord's strength, we had nothing to fear. We knew that the authorities were always looking for anything they could use against us. Sometimes they didn't need to have a reason, except that we followed Jesus.

Three weeks ago, on the day of the Lord Jesus Christ, Sunday, we gathered as usual. After receiving the Eucharist and giving thanks, the doors burst open and soldiers rushed in.

Claudius tried to protect the remaining Eucharist reserved for the sick. But a soldier struck him in the neck with his sword. Those who resisted were slain on the spot. Even the children, so innocent, were run through because of their tears.

Marcellus was spared because, by the grace of God, he was out visiting the sick. So many of our number lay dead on the floor and out in the street.

Upon restraining me, they began hitting and kicking me in my helplessness. Nearly unconscious, I discovered as I lay on the floor that some of the Eucharist was under my shoulder. Slowly I shifted so that my face was over It and I was able to consume my Lord's Precious Body. My eyes searched for more, but because they were nearly swollen shut, it was hard to see.

Suddenly the soldiers grabbed me and dragged my broken body outside. Those who had been spared death were tied like cattle and thrown into a wagon. The women huddled together seeking poor comfort, their clothes having been ripped from them.

All were covered in blood, bruised, beaten and swollen.

I raised my voice and prayed, "Lord Jesus, receive Your loving children into Your loving embrace. May Your mercy. . . ." Someone hit my head and I did not awaken until much later in this place of imprisonment.

Since I've been here, so many have gone to their death. Some have gone singing and praising the Lord, while others simply and silently pray, focusing on Jesus.

In our cell there are seventy-eight men, women and children. Originally our cell numbered two hundred six. The children would gather around me and the adults behind them. We prayed and talked about Jesus and how wonderful it will be to go to Him.

Little Sara was left behind when both of her parents died martyrs' deaths. She was eleven years in this world and one year in grace. Sara jumped up and exclaimed, "Mamma and Daddy are with Jesus in Heaven! I'm happy that I will be with them. I'm not afraid because Jesus will take me to Heaven." She was so wise and filled with faith.

When the soldiers came for her, she wasn't sad or afraid. She held the guard's hand and smiled at him, saying, "Are you taking me to meet Jesus and Mommy and Daddy?" The guard's eyes began to fill with tears. He looked at me and softly said, "I'm so sorry!" Little Sara had touched his heart. The guard's name is Fabian. He is the one who provided these writing utensils for me to jot down these humble remembrances of a priest of Christ.

Yesterday a soldier came to inspect the garrison. We were on his inspection list as well. He came into the cell after asking those with him to remain outside. He was a centurion whose face looked familiar to me. He was not cold as the others and his eyes searched the prisoners' faces. Finally, he saw me and slowly walked toward me. The closer he came, the more I realized that our paths had crossed before.

The centurion stopped in front of me, viewing this broken body before him. You see, when they attacked us, they broke both my legs and one arm. My legs are twisted; one faces the opposite direction. In my chest is an open wound, infested with the insects and maggots that have taken it as their home.

He looked in my eyes and whispered, "Simon? Simon? Is that you? Are you not the one who carried His cross? Do you not know me? I am he who *made* you carry His cross and later pierced His side when He hung there lifeless. I am Longinus."

I remembered him now. It was he who had said, "Surely, this was the Son of God."

Longinus continued to speak, quietly, softly: "If I could take you out of here, I would do so this very moment. Is there anything I *can* do?"

After inquiring how he knew I was here, I told him that my notes must get out.

Marcellus had received word that a certain centurion was looking for Simon. Although he was not a Christian, he was a sympathizer. It was said that Mother Mary herself directed him to Cyrene. Marcellus met with him under cover of night and told him of the events.

I told Longinus about the friendship that Fabian had provided and asked if perhaps they would help me to get my notes to Marcellus, who in turn would bring them to my cousin Jacob. Before leaving me, he agreed.

So now I must finish whatever I can. As you may realize, Jacob, it is most difficult to write, so I pray you will be able to decipher this. Fabian has just come in to ask that I let him know when I have completed this journal. He tells me: "When they come for you, I cannot gain time for you. Once I retrieve your notes, they will go to Longinus, who in turn will deliver them to whomever you wish. Please hurry."

Now, Jacob, I write my last thoughts, not only for you but for all who read these words. (From Simon's final letter to his cousin Jacob)

Like the Apostles, we are now commanded to go out, and we cannot exclude anyone from the Good News. To be saved, we must be extensions of the Savior. To be raised up, we must raise others up to Him. This is no easy task. It is no mere matter of publishing a message. It must be made effective, and this is a challenge to overwhelm the strongest of men and women. It is a message freely given to the free, and it must be freely received.

Jesus implied that the flesh itself was not prepared to hear it. He said that we needed the Spirit to prepare us for the real truths we must face! Like the Apostles before Pentecost, we look for earthly kingdoms, for immediate success, for tangible rewards, for material victories. We tend to count Christian success in those most unchristian terms: money, property, prosperity, political power, great emotions, friends, comforts. These are the earmarks of worldly success. Is it not true that the Lord must say to us, as He once said to the Eleven: *"I have yet many things to say to you: but you cannot bear them now."* (John 16:12)

When shall we be able to bear them? For until we do learn to bear the truth and live by it very personally and concretely, we are not bringing the Good News to the world.

Jesus assured us that as His Apostles and Disciples, His missionaries of today and tomorrow, many souls await our arrival: *"The harvest indeed is great, but the labourers are few."* (Luke 10:2)

Much is required of the Lord's laborers if our work is to be effective. We must be emptied of self and filled with Christ. Our hearts must be opened that God's Presence may fill them. Jesus rejoins on all of us Christians to pray God for more apostles of great zeal and holiness. He exhorts us to pray to the Owner of the harvest to send out laborers to reap it.

Although the harvest is great and plentiful, and the Owner sends out laborers to gather it in, the enemies of man are always busy, and there is continual danger to the good work of God's servants. Persecution, disappointments, and even death may await the men and women of God. Thus Jesus reminds us, *"Go: Behold I send you as lambs among wolves."* (Luke 10:3)

In these words, the Lord Who is all wisdom spells out our Christian vocation. It is one of both joy and sorrow; of success and failure; of an abundant harvest; of wolves ever ready to devour the unsuspecting lambs. Indeed, such will be the history of Christ's Church, as prophesied by Himself.

We rejoice at the great courage and charity of the saints of God. We are sad at the spectacle of ignorance, bad will, rejection, hatred and cruelty on the part of our persecutors. We are glad at the spread of Christ's kingdom on earth, for all the good things brought by faith and the love of Christ. We sorrow at the many who remain blind and cold at the news of their Redemption.

These hard paradoxes are the mystery of Christianity, the mystery of human freedom, and human weakness, the mystery of God's ways with man.

May God enlighten our minds and open our hearts, so that His new gifts and renewed graces may always find room in us.

And now, Jacob, I go to meet my Lord and Savior, Jesus Christ, with Whom I will spend my eternity. Amen.

Your cousin,

Simon, a priest of Christ
For The Glory Of God

(From Simon's final letter to his cousin Jacob)

Epilogue

Marcellus," Jacob said, "words cannot express my gratitude for the sacrifice you made and the dangers you faced to deliver this testament to me. How can I possibly reward your heroic efforts? Please, tell me how Simon died. Was any mercy given him?"

"Fabian the guard was an eye witness to his martyrdom, as was Longinus the Centurion. Both have since been baptized in Christ. I will tell you what they told me.

"After Simon called to me to remove his writings," Fabian related, "he fell deeply into prayer. But many of those who were in his cell needed comfort, and so he painfully dragged his broken body over to comfort them. He blessed them, performed unions, baptized, anointed and ministered to all.

"In the rolled sleeve of his garment, he had hidden some of the Eucharistic Bread that he had managed to retrieve from the floor at the time of his arrest. He prayed the prayers of the Lord's Supper and then crawled to each person, giving them but a small crumb of this Eucharist. How there was enough to go around, only the Lord knows. When all had received, he gave thanks. It was then that they came for him.

"They grabbed hold of him and demanded that he stand. He tried but his legs were useless. Then they kicked his legs, laughing at the weakling before them. Someone said, 'So your God cannot help you now. Your Christ is dead, and you, too, will die as He did. Look at this piece of worthless trash. No one can save you.'

"Just then he looked up to Heaven and declared, 'Look! Jesus is waiting for His servant with outstretched arms. My soul I shall place in His hands. You may have this useless body for I no longer have need of it.'

"The guards were not only amazed at his words, but at his appearance, for suddenly all his pain seemed to leave his body, and a beautiful peace and serenity overtook him. They let go of

97

him and he fell to the floor as if falling onto a soft pillow. Then another guard yelled from the door of the cell: 'Drag that slime to his fate — the fate that awaits all traitors of Caesar.'

"So, they dragged him off by his broken and twisted legs, his head bouncing on the hard stone floor. The other prisoners for Christ sang hymns of praise and Psalms of help.

"Simon was taken to the courtyard and thrown into a huge pit where bears waited for their new play thing. Fabian said that after he was thrown into the pit, Simon managed to stand. He raised both arms to Heaven and praised God and His Son, Jesus Christ. He claimed that there was a bright light surrounding him. It was so blinding that they could not witness his death.

"When it was over, they found him dismembered, his body parts strewn among the beasts. Simon is now in Heaven."

Jacob turned to Marcellus. Although tears ran down his face, it was bathed in the light of an indescribably joyful peace. "Marcellus," he said, "I, too, want to be a Christian. I want to serve Christ all the days of my life."

> *I will praise thee, O Lord, with my whole heart:*
> *for thou hast heard the words of my mouth.*
> *I will sing praise to thee in the sight of the angels:*
> *I will worship towards thy holy temple,*
> *and I will give glory to thy name.*
> *For thy mercy, and for thy truth:*
> *for thou hast magnified thy holy name above all*
> *In what day soever I shall call upon thee, hear me:*
> *thou shalt mutiply strength in my soul.*

(Psalm 137:1-3)

ALL SCRIPTURE REFERENCES FROM:

THE
HOLY BIBLE

TRANSLATED FROM THE LATIN VULGATE

DILIGENTLY COMPARED WITH THE HEBREW, GREEK, AND OTHER EDITIONS
IN DIVERS LANGUAGES

THE OLD TESTAMENT

FIRST PUBLISHED BY THE ENGLISH, COLLEGE AT DOUAY, A.D. 1609

AND

THE NEW TESTAMENT

FIRST PUBLISHED BY THE ENGLISH COLLEGE AT RHEIMS, A.D. 1582

*WITH ANNOTATIONS, REFERENCES, AND AN HISTORICAL AND
CHRONOLOGICAL INDEX*

THE WHOLE REVISED AND DILIGENTLY COMPARED
WITH THE LATIN VULGATE
BY BISHOP RICHARD CHALLONER, A.D. 1749-1752

HIS EMINENCE JAMES CARDINAL GIBBONS

ARCHBISHOP OF BALTIMORE

TAN BOOKS AND PUBLISHERS, INC.
Rockford, Illinois 61105

Title Description of Books by CMJ Associates, INC.

Behold the Man, Simon of Cyrene By Father Martin DePorres

Inspired writing by a gifted new Author. This story shows us the
gifts given to Simon. Throught carrying the Cross with Jesus,
Simon shares with us the gifts we can expect by carrying our
daily crosses. $12.25

Becoming the Handmaid of the Lord By Dr. Ronda Chervin

The journals of this well known Catholic writer span her family
life as wife and mother, mystical graces sustaining her through
a mid-life crisis, the suicide of her beloved son, her widowhood
and finally a Religious Sister at the age of 58. Insightful, inspiring
& challenging. 327 pages of the heart. $13.75

Ties that Bind By Ronda Chervin

The story of a Marriage. This beautiful novel presents the wife's point
of view and the husbands point of view on the same conflict. The
author Dr. Chervin has written many books on Catholic life. *Ties that
Bind* is both funny and inspiring. A great gift for couple thinking
about marriage as well. $ 8.50

The Cheese Stands Alone By David Craig

(The formost religious poet of the day) A dynamite account of a radi-
cal conversion from the world of drugs to the search for holiness in
the Catholic Church. Realism & poetic imagery combine to make this
a must for those who want the real thing. Its a rare book that both
monastic and charismatic — anyone acquainted with the latter will
love the chapter on misguided zeal, aptly titled "Busbey Burkeley." $12.50

The History of Eucharistic Adoration By Father John Hardon, S.J.

In an age of widespread confusion and disbelief, this document offers
unprecedented clarity in the most important element of our faith. I
recommend that it be prayerfully studied and widely circulated. It is
thoroughly researched and well documented, and promises to enlight
en, instruct and inspire countless souls to an undying love of our
Eucharistic Lord. $ 4.00

The Bishop Sheen We Knew By Father Albert Shamon

A booklet filled with little known information from his Vicar, Fr.
Albert J.M. Shamon, Bishop Dennis Hickey and Fr. Mike Hogan,
the three remaining priests who worked under Bishop Sheen. A
chance to see the day to day workings of the acknowledged prophet
of our times. $ 4.00

To order additional copies of this book:

Please complete the form below and send for each copy

CMJ Associates, Inc.
P.O. Box 661 • Oak Lawn, IL 60454
call 708-636-2995 or fax 708-636-2855
email jwby@aol.com

Name _____

Address _____

City _____ State _____ Zip _____

Phone ( ) _____

	PRICE EA.	QUAN.	SUBTOTAL
Behold the Man!	$12.25 x	____	= $_____
Becoming the Handmaid of the Lord	$13.75 x	____	= $_____
Ties that Bind	$ 8.50 x	____	= $_____
The Cheese Stands Alone	$12.50 x	____	= $_____
The History of Eucharistic Adoration	$ 4.00 x	____	= $_____
The Bishop Sheen We Knew	$ 4.00 x	____	= $_____
By Way of the Cross	$12.25 x	____	= $_____
Lost in the World	$12.50 x	____	= $_____
Dancing with God . . .	$12.50 x	____	= $_____

+ tax (for Illinois residents only) = $_____

+ 15% for S & H = $_____

TOTAL = $_____

☐ Check # _____ ☐ Visa ☐ MasterCard Exp. Date ___/___/___

Card #_____

Signature _____

Many new & exciting releases for Winter 1997

*(If you are interested in any or all of these exciting new titles send us
your name and address and we can send you a notice of publication with the price.)*

By Way of the Cross By Carol J. Ross

Autobiography. When you read *By Way of the Cross* you will open
yourself to tears of empathy and of joy as you see this woman struggling with terribly physical and mental crosses, scooped up into
breathtaking visions of the supernatural world.
Paperback. Full color photos. 468 pages. $12.25

Lost in the World: Found in Christ By Father Christopher Scadron

The story of a priest ordained at the age of 63 — As a young Jewish
man Padre Pio predicated he would become a Priest. After years of
floundering and sin as a naval officer and an artist, this unsually gifted and interesting man became a priest at 63! A tale all Catholics will
find moving and deeply inspiring, it is also a must gift for any man
you know who might be called to the priesthood at an age older than
the usual. $12.50

Dancing with God through the Evening of Life
By Mary Anne McCrickard Benas

Unique insight into the world of the hospice worker and the patient
relationship. The beautiful faithful outlook of a elderly man dying
and the gifts he gives us through this experience. $12.50

The Third Millennium Women By Patricia Hershwitzky

Consider the sinking feeling many Catholics get when they see litera-
ture about preparing for this great event. They expect what they read
or pretend to read to be true, but dull as dishwater. By contrast —
here is a book that is wildly funny and also profound. Written by a
"revert" (born Catholic who left and then returned), it is also ideal as
a gift for those many women we know are teetering on the verge of
returning Home.

Messages to the World from the Mother of God

Daily meditative pocketsize prayer book on the monthly messages
given the visionaries in Medjugorji for the conversion of the World,
back to her son Jesus. These messages for the World started in 1984
till the present. In 1987 the messages began on the 25th of the month
(union of two hearts with the 5 wounds of Jesus) thus the 25th. These
are from St. James Church in Medjugorji. Great Gift!!! $11.50

Children of the Breath By Martin Chervin

Who would have dared to challenge Creation if, at the close of each
new day, God said, "It is perfect." Instead, His lips spoke "It is
good . . ." and the serpent was already in Eden. Thus begins *Children
of the Breath*, a startling journey into the desert where Christ was
tempted for forty days of darkness and light. With immense clarity,
lyricism, and humor, author Martin Chervin has delivered a power-
house that will engage readers of any faith.